Pizzazz

A View From The Obelisk
Roman Fever
Pizzazz

Hugh Leonard

A SAMUEL FRENCH ACTING EDITION

SAMUEL FRENCH

FOUNDED 1830

SAMUELFRENCH.COM
SAMUELFRENCH-LONDON.CO.UK

ISBN 978-0-573-01641-7

www.SamuelFrench.com
www.SamuelFrench-London.co.uk

FOR PRODUCTION ENQUIRIES

UNITED STATES AND CANADA

Info@SamuelFrench.com

1-866-598-8449

UNITED KINGDOM AND EUROPE

Plays@SamuelFrench-London.co.uk

020-7255-4302/01

Each title is subject to availability from Samuel French, depending upon country of performance. Please be aware that *PIZZAZZ* may not be licensed by Samuel French in your territory. Professional and amateur producers should contact the nearest Samuel French office or licensing partner to verify availability.

CONTENTS

AUTHOR'S NOTE

Pizzazz consists of three plays intended solely as entertainment. If they have a theme in common, it is that each one deals with travellers—in Rome, near Dublin, and on the Shannon—who are apart from their natural environment. Another quality in common is perhaps suggested by the original composite title *Scorpions*. As for the individual plays, *A View from the Obelisk* is a reworking and expansion of a 25-minute play I wrote for television sixteen years ago: only the situation and the theme are unchanged. *Roman Fever* is adapted from Edith Wharton's whiplash story; a gem which, rightly or wrongly, I thought cried out to be put on a stage. As for *Pizzazz*, I have always wanted to write the dramatic equivalent of a Chinese Box: the toy that is simple to look upon and drives one to near-madness when played with. This is my attempt, and I hope it is not as intimidating to see as it was to write.

Hugh Leonard

A View from the Obelisk

CHARACTERS

Owen
Rosemary
The Boy, Eoghain

A VIEW FROM THE OBELISK*

A hilltop. Afternoon

We are at the base of an obelisk which is built on the summit; the upper part tapers above us out of sight. An arched alcove is set into the base, with a bench running across its width. We may assume that the other three sides of the base are identical. There are no trees, just grass and outcrops of stone. A sense of space

Owen and Rosemary come into view, he leading the way even though the climb has used up much of his strength. He is in his late forties, clothes well-cut. Rosemary is forty; she looks younger; a Londoner

Rosemary Darling, do slow down, these aren't walking shoes. (*Out of breath*) Shouldn't we turn back?
Owen Look. (*He indicates the obelisk*)
Rosemary We're here then? Clever us.
Owen And there's the view. This is the place.

Rosemary laughs

What?
Rosemary You looked as if you were going to genuflect. "This is the place."
Owen I was quoting.
Rosemary Oh, yes?
Owen Brigham Young. When he and his followers looked down on the Great Salt Lake.
Rosemary All those wives. How many did he have?
Owen God knows. One's enough for anyone.
Rosemary But not for some.
Owen Now, now.
Rosemary (*as she puts her arm through his, smiling*) Couldn't resist it.
Owen Look at the view.
Rosemary It's pretty.
Owen Is that all? Pretty?
Rosemary Impressive.
Owen Over there, Wicklow. (*Turning from right to left*) The mountains, Kattygollagher, the two Sugarloafs, Bray Head. There, the sea.
Rosemary (*clowning*) Is it? Oh, good.

---

* N.B. Paragraph 3 on page ii of this Acting Edition regarding photocopying and video-recording should be carefully read.

Owen Vico, Sorrento Point, the island. On clear days you can make out Snowdonia or the Mournes to the north. Walk around here, you can see Dublin.

Rosemary Have a heart, I'm out of puff.

Owen Pretty, she says. It's terrific.

Rosemary giggles

Now what?

Rosemary "Turrific." You're getting your brogue back.

Owen A brogue is a shoe. If you mean my accent, I've always had it. Why not?

Rosemary It's thickening. I mean it. Since yesterday, since we got off the plane. Congealing by the minute.

Owen That is not true.

Rosemary "Dat is not troo." You see? I don't mind, I like it. It was what attracted me.

Owen When?

Rosemary Then. I have to sit. I'm not the hill-climber I thought I was.

Owen Who's the invalid now?

Rosemary Smug.

Owen grins and looks at the view. His attitude is of one consciously and aggressively alive

(*Without rancour*) Yes, pleased with yourself. I think I liked you better when you were ill. Well, you watch it, my lad. You're not out of the woods yet.

Owen (*unconcerned*) Mm-hmm.

Rosemary "This day will end in tears."

Owen Come again?

Rosemary When I was little and we were laughing too much, high spirits and so on, that was my grandmother's pet phrase. She had one for all occasions ... could have made a fortune in greetings cards. And the day always did end in tears.

Owen So?

Rosemary What I'm trying to say is, slow ... down. Please?

Owen I'm fine.

Rosemary The sort you are, you give convalescence a bad name. I hadn't unpacked last night before you were off to look up your old cronies. It could have waited.

Owen We agree there.

Rosemary It was too much for you ... I knew.

Owen I don't mean it that way. I met them ...

Rosemary You said.

Owen George Furlong, Charlie Duggan and Suffering God.

Rosemary Who?

Owen His name is Sean Cronin, but he used to preface every second statement with "Oh, suffering God". In our town we all had nicknames.

Rosemary What was yours?

Owen Oh, no. You're thrifty . . . you'd save it for future use. Well, I wasn't expecting a brass band or a light in anyone's window. A few maudlin reminiscences would have done.

Rosemary You said you'd had a good time.

Owen I thought I'd had. It was like walking away from an accident: it isn't until later you notice the blood. I said to George Furlong: "Do you remember above on the Burma Road during the freeze-up of forty-seven. We were tobogganing and Sergeant Lawlor stood in front of us and held his hand up as if he were stopping a motor car. We thought we'd killed him." George looked me in the eye, smiled and said: "I disremember that."

Rosemary Perhaps he did.

Owen Not he. Oh, there were salutations and "How are things in Limeyland?" and "Weren't you the wise man to get out of this kip". Charlie Duggan went home after one drink, sucking a peppermint. Suffering God stayed and got pissed. All three of them were as unchanged as a snapshot. But it was as if the past—theirs and mine—was a club, and I'd broken the rules.

Rosemary You do dramatize.

Owen No re-admission.

Rosemary A hilltop is all it takes. Put you on the summit and you're King Lear.

Owen scowls

You say yourself they were civil.

Owen Civility may be sign of friendship in Highgate. Here, it's the opposite.

Rosemary I see. If they were really your friends, they'd have killed you.

Owen (*not heavily*) Dry up.

Rosemary Charming.

Owen It was because I was the one who got away, who escaped. That's not forgiven.

Rosemary There are worse sins.

Owen Such as?

Rosemary I mean, face it, darling, you left more than just a country.

He looks at her, feigning lack of comprehension

Let's not play the innocent. What about Moira? Perhaps your friends' coolness had just a little to do with her.

Owen (*dismissive*) No.

Rosemary Why not? You're forever telling me how religious they all are. No divorce, no living in sin.

Owen That's in the past. Nowadays they pay lip-service to the rules, but it's on the surface. Around here, in the towns, they've changed.

Rosemary How would you know?

Owen I read, I stay in touch. The world finally got in at them.

Rosemary Well done, world! Where does she live?

Again, he looks at her with studied blankness

Moira.

Owen You know.
Rosemary I mean, from here.

He goes upstage, looks off, then turns his back on what he is describing

Owen Look out that way. You see the two long piers? That's Dun
Laoghaire. Go inland from the far one and there's a maze of houses . . .
off-white walls and red roofs.
Rosemary I see it.
Owen Funny . . . all the way from here to Dublin, nothing but roof-tops. It
wasn't like this when I left . . . there were patches of green. Now they're
spreading like molasses.
Rosemary Like what?
Owen W. C. Fields. "Molasses . . . spreadingest stuff I ever did see!"
Rosemary You should visit her.
Owen What for?
Rosemary I wouldn't mind.
Owen Liar.
Rosemary Really. I'm sure she's curious . . . I would be. She'll want to know
that you've been ill, that you're getting better now . . .
Owen Yes, first the good news, then the bad. No, thanks.
Rosemary What you mean is, seeing her might upset you.
Owen Guilty conscience?
Rosemary *You* tell *me.*
Owen Wouldn't you say it's a bit late in the day for putting me to the test?
Rosemary How?
Owen Trial by ordeal. Like giving money to an orphan and sending him to
the shops to see if he can be trusted. I thought I'd won my spurs years ago
. . . came home with the change, whiter than white.
Rosemary So you have. Sorr-ee!
Owen What is there to prove? It's dead, all done with. Gone . . . yes?
Rosemary Yes. You see, I never realized we'd get this close to it . . . to her. I
mean, she's down there now. And I wish it was tomorrow and we were on
the train for the west.
Owen Fool.
Rosemary *(nodding, meaning herself)* Idiot.
Owen Anyway, I'm not a masochist. I don't enjoy having doors slammed in
my face. And if it wasn't slammed . . . *(In a voice quivering with female
outrage)* "Can you credit it, Dympna, after all these years, not caring
whether a body was alive or dead, as God is me judge he had the audacity
to come begging for forgiveness."

As Rosemary looks at him:

Well, I wouldn't, no fear, but she'd say I did . . . not married to an artist
for nothing. "But I gave him his answer. I told that blackguard, I
said——" *(He breaks off. His attempt at mockery has perhaps come too
close to home)* I . . . told him——
Rosemary Leave it.

Owen (*a new tack, as if to destroy the thought*) Listen, that woman, tidy? . . . don't talk to me. On the mantelpiece . . . two vases, right? Their distance from the exact centre measured with a ha'penny ruler.

Rosemary (*laughing*) You are wicked.

Owen God's truth. And every object in between balanced for size and symmetry. Because if the ornaments were *not* symmetrical, then the walls would fly apart, the floors open up and the world collapse.

Rosemary Dreadful man.

Owen As a matter of awful fact, Moira does believe—or at least she did—that the world will end in the year Two Thousand.

Rosemary You're making this up.

Owen No, really. It's not an uncommon belief in these parts. The Irish believe that not only does God move in mysterious ways but in round numbers. That's the reason their money went metric.

Rosemary Oh, stop.

Owen I swear it. They—— (*He stops*)

Rosemary They what? Are you all right?

Owen A bit . . . light-headed. It'll pass. (*Something has happened within him. His reaction is part bewilderment, part fear*)

Rosemary You look awful. Sit by me.

Owen No . . .

Rosemary I say yes. (*She draws him to her*) Your hand is like ice. How do you feel?

Owen (*an attempt at a grin*) Not well.

Rosemary (*alarmed*) You were overdoing it . . . I told you.

Owen The damnedest feeling, as if I'd gone hollow inside. Wow.

Rosemary Have you come over faint, is that it?

He shakes his head

You're so stubborn. You turn what's supposed to be a convalescence into a holiday. You go climbing mountains.

Owen A hill. One hill.

Rosemary It was stupid.

Owen Yes, it was.

Rosemary And I'm worse. Instead of helping, I nag. Should I go for a doctor.

Owen No, wait. It's easing.

Rosemary Are you sure?

Owen Give me a minute. Do you know, I think just now I nearly died.

Rosemary (*frightened*) I never know when you're exaggerating and when you aren't.

Owen It was like going off the edge of a cliff . . . all you had to do was let go. Nothing to it. Something happened to me. I mean, something isn't the same as it was.

Rosemary Look, you wait here . . .

Owen There's no need. It's gone.

Rosemary (*sceptical*) Just like that?

Owen We'll give it a few minutes, then we can start back.

Rosemary Are you quite mad?
Owen It's downhill, and the hotel's not far.
Rosemary You're going to sit here and rest——
Owen I just said so.
Rosemary—and I'm going to walk down to the village——
Owen No doctors.
Rosemary —and telephone to the hotel for a car.
Owen There's no need.
Rosemary Meanwhile, I want you to promise me you'll stay here quietly.
And if you won't, I'll leave you. I'll fly back to London, I mean it.
Owen No, you don't.

As she looks at him:

I promise.
Rosemary I'll be back in fifteen minutes. Now stay.

She turns to look at him, concerned. He nods

She goes off

Left on his own, he sits for a moment, then stands experimentally, gauging his own reaction. He feels his pulse

Eoghain appears around the corner of the obelisk. He moves slowly, engrossed in comparing his sketch of the panorama on a drawing pad with the reality. He holds up the pad, not noticing Owen. He is young, thin, poorly dressed

Owen watches him

Eoghain (*in disgust*) Ah, feck.
Owen Language!

Eoghain whirls around, startled

Afternoon.
Eoghain Sorry.
Owen What for? Like yourself, I thought I was the only one up here.
Eoghain I was just——
Owen Sketching. So I see.

Eoghain is ill at ease. He looks from the sketch pad to the view without seeing either

Nothing more embarrassing. I've been through it. You think you're alone, so you make faces or let loose a few adjectives. Then you find you're under surveillance.

Pause

Are you from around here?
Eoghain Beg pardon?
Owen I asked if you were——
Eoghain I'm from the town.

Owen Snap. I mean, I was originally. Not a bad little place.
Eoghain Suppose not.
Owen To get out of. (*Chattily*) I've been away fifteen years. I'd forgotten how magnificent the view was. Just like you, I'd come here and sit. Sometimes I'd bring a sketch pad. We all did. (*He senses that Eoghain is uncomfortable*) I'm not, by the way, the sort of gentleman who prowls around lonely places. If you know what I mean.
Eoghain (*unable to cope*) Pardon?
Owen (*hand upraised*) Word of honour.
Eoghain (*mumbling*) I don't mind.
Owen (*amused*) Don't you? . . . bravo. (*Then*) No, there was very definitely a lady wife here just now. She ran off on an errand of mercy. Aid for the afflicted.

Eoghain nods, uncomprehending. As he turns away:

I've been ill, you see. And after what happened a minute ago, I thought the old saying was about to come true . . . "Long life and . . ." You know it.
Eoghain ". . . agus bas in nEireann." Death in Ireland.
Owen That's it. Well, the latter part of it, anyway: I'm not quite your aged pensioner. (*Confidentially*) I had a bit of a fright.
Eoghain If you want me to, I could go and get——
Owen No, I'm quite recovered. My wife is fetching a car of some sort . . . out of fussiness, not necessity. Look . . . apologies. My deliverance made me talkative. First time I ever knew what *joie de vivre* meant.
Eoghain Pardon?
Owen "There's night and day, brother, both sweet things. Sun, moon and stars, brother, all sweet things." I was quoting.
Eoghain I know. "Lavengro" by George Borrow.
Owen (*surprised*) Yes.
Eoghain Nice book. Shocking anti-Catholic, but.
Owen (*blinking*) Just so. At any rate, I apologize. You press on.
Eoghain I think I'll leave it. The light's gone. (*He tears the page from his sketch pad and crumples it, throwing it away*)
Owen Don't destroy it.
Eoghain It's awful.

As Owen retrieves it:

What are you at?
Owen Really, are there no litter laws? (*Smoothing it out*) What have we here? Yes . . . Da Vinci strikes again.
Eoghain (*becoming annoyed*) Excuse me, but that's——
Owen Private. It can't be done, can it?
Eoghain What?
Owen That view of the bay. No-one has ever got the sweep of the hills and that sky and sea. I know I never could. Not bad, though . . . not an abomination. May I? (*He takes Eoghain's pencil and sketch pad*)
Eoghain Them's mine.

Owen *These are* yours. No, you've missed it ... but everybody does: even Corot couldn't catch those lines. But you go at it like a miser.

Eoghain It's only a rough sketch.

Owen It is now ... it didn't set out to be. (*Sketching very quickly*) For one thing, you should use a softer lead. All this is good for is ticking off winners on a racing sheet.

Eoghain I can't aff——

Owen Then steal one. And go at it like this, like a drunkard. And use the long muscle, the one from the eyes through the brain to the pencil. Hang on ... there we are: there's your skyline.

Eoghain (*looking*) Jasus.

Owen You approve?

Eoghain It's smashin'.

Owen Don't confuse tricks with talent. It's still wrong.

Eoghain *I* couldn't do it.

Owen It's a question of rearrangement, and you can't rearrange those mountains. They don't play fair. Take your eyes off them and they move around, they change colour, they cheat.

Eoghain I bet you're an artist.

Owen Think so? And I bet you want to become one.

Eoghain I'm going to.

Owen I'm sure.

Eoghain See if I don't.

Owen No doubt of it. And if I smiled, it was at a certain familiar note of determination.

Eoghain (*defensive*) Don't see an'thin' wrong in that.

Owen Nor do I ... bravely said. What kind of artist?

Eoghain Pardon?

Owen Apart from being a great one. Oriental ladies with purple skins? Elephant stampedes? Tiny tots with eyes like soup plates? Or perhaps you favour the far end of the spectrum ... pictures no-one understands: "Puce Upon Puce" or "Reclining Parallelogram". Abstracts are always a hit with the critics. You see, if you confuse or bore them, they assume your intellect to be mightier than theirs, and just to be on the safe side they use words like "disturbing", "innovative" and "exuberant". Of course between that sort of art and the purple ladies there's a world of choice. Any preferences?

Eoghain simply stares at him, hardly comprehending, but aware that he is the butt of Owen's hostile wit

I say, you're hardly starved for choice.

Eoghain (*mumbling*) Don't follow you.

Owen Didn't quite hear. Say again.

Eoghain Are you pickin' on me?

Owen Pickin'?

Eoghain Makin' a jeer.

Owen Of you?

Eoghain Just ... lay off.

Owen Have I offended?
Eoghain Too bloody full o' yourself. I'm goin' for me tea.
Owen Wait. (*Sincerely*) *Mea culpa* ... sorry, lad. Let's blame it on the altitude. At six hundred feet nerves reach breaking point. Or let's say that I was shit-scared and wanted to take it out on someone.
Eoghain No call for bein' rude.
Owen None. So go for your tea.
Eoghain What was up with you?
Owen Up?
Eoghain When you were sick.
Owen (*tapping his chest*) Heart.
Eoghain Oh, yeah.
Owen It was making queer noises. Don't be alarmed ... *strange* noises. So they fixed it. Opened me up and put a valve in.
Eoghain (*incredulous*) They what?
Owen Just like changing a spark plug.
Eoghain (*grinning*) Feck off.
Owen Sorry?
Eoghain Pull the other one.
Owen A small plastic valve. Does that strike you as comical.
Eoghain Into your ticker?
Owen Of course.
Eoghain (*his grin fading*) Are you havin' another go?
Owen How?
Eoghain At me. Hearts gettin' ... operated on!
Owen You're the most hypersensitive young man I've ever met. (*Wearily*) Oh, God. (*He takes a cautious look from left to right, then unbuttons his shirt*) This could be misinterpreted.
Eoghain What are you at?
Owen Ye of little faith.

Like Owen, Eoghain peers nervously about, then looks at Owen's chest

Eoghain Jasus.
Owen Doubting Thomas! (*Buttoning up*) Where have you been hiding yourself? These days doctors do it in their sleep. I wonder if mine did ... ?
Eoghain Like a tin o' sardines, what?
Owen Pardon?
Eoghain They opened you. Bloody good.
Owen Isn't it! You did hear, didn't you, about the moon landings?

Eoghain laughs heartily

Not to mention the microchip.
Eoghain Very tasty. Oh, you're a queer harp.

He laughs again. Owen joins in, glancing at him a trifle uneasily, not sure whether Eoghain is laughing at him or with him

Owen At any rate, I'm on the mend.
Eoghain Grand.

Owen So when does it start? I mean this artistic breakthrough. Do you still live at home?

Eoghain Yes. Look, if you're——

Owen I'm interested. With your parents?

Eoghain Yeah.

Owen That's nice for them. And you work at something?

Eoghain In an office.

Owen Clerking. That's not so bad: I've done some of it in my time. And you'd be what? Twenty?

Eoghain Goin' on for.

Owen I envy you. It's a wonderful age ... later on, I mean. As in heart surgery, distance lends enchantment. Look, I don't mean to seem a wet blanket, but try not to leave it too late.

Eoghain How?

Owen To get out. Out of here.

Eoghain I'm goin' to.

Owen When? Tomorrow? Next year?

Eoghain There's still tucks of time. Your man ... the French fella. He was a painter. (*Uncertain*) Gogg ...

Owen Van Gogh?

Eoghain (*shaking his head*) South Sea Islands.

Owen Gauguin. I take your point. He didn't desert his wife and children until he was in his thirties ... but then he was a genius. Are you? Sacrificing yourself is easy: what's food, cooked and on the table, or a bed made up, ready to fall into? Trimmings, that's all ... nets to hold us. But sacrificing other people, being thought a blackguard, that's where nerve comes in.

Eoghain I'll go, never fear.

Owen Watch out for the nets.

Eoghain I think you're at me again.

Owen Me?

Eoghain (*grumbling*) Sittin' there and actin' ... actin' so ...

Owen You aren't long on what they call word power, are you?

Eoghain Just ... buzz off. I was here first. You buzz off an' leave me alone.

Owen I promised to wait.

Eoghain Fella can't even draw in peace.

Owen (*correcting him*) Sketch.

Eoghain Dry up.

Owen Perhaps it's because you touched a nerve. You said: "I bet you're an artist." Well, you lose your bet. I had ambitions once, but wouldn't it be awful if you were right, if I'd had more than just a knack. No, I doubt it. There isn't an Irishman living who doesn't believe he could be a genius if only someone would lend him a pencil. It's our strength and our frailty: we're convinced that all our cygnets are swans.

Eoghain (*grinning*) You're gas.

Owen Gas ... *bag*, more like. You press on: don't mind me.

Eoghain I'll get there.

Owen Perhaps. But I meant what I said: delay is death.

Eoghain Yeah. It's not so easy.
Owen No.
Eoghain You see, I'm the only one at home. People bring you into the world; you can't just walk off and leave them.
Owen You will, someday.
Eoghain Oh, sure. Only it takes a kind of, I dunno ... hardness ... not caring about them. How do I know what brave is: to run off or stay here and hang on to the job? I suppose what counts is how good I am.
Owen How good *are* you?
Eoghain Dunno. What do you think?
Owen Who am I? ... a stranger. You ask yourself, and if the answer's the one you want to hear, then all it takes is the price of a mailboat ticket.

Eoghain laughs silently, shaking his head

Yes?
Eoghain Nothin'. It's just the way words come out of you. Everythin' like oil, not a lump or bubble in it. I can't stick one sentence after the other.
Owen You just did.
Eoghain You're not really from the town, are you?
Owen Born and bred.
Eoghain I know ... from outa one o' them big houses on the Vico.
Owen I lived in a corporation house off Castle Street.
Eoghain That's where I——
Owen With my parents. My accent and what you call the way words come out of me ... they aren't assumed. They were acquired.
Eoghain In England.
Owen And in America. Like you, I came up here to sketch. I went to the evening classes. A teacher bestowed on me that adjective that is the teething-ring of the arts: "promising". I was offered a scholarship, but I had my living to make and couldn't accept it. So I waited. I thought that given time, my parents would disappear. Not die ... nothing so cruel, but vanish magically, cease to exist. And I would be free: no more obligations, no ties, no guilt. The miracle refused to happen. Parents can be such obdurate creatures.
Eoghain But you got away.
Owen I met a girl: a warm, sweet-natured person named Moira.
Eoghain And she was rich.
Owen I didn't know you were a romantic. No, she wasn't rich. We went to the Tech together, or rather simultaneously. I was studying art; she favoured domestic science. A bad omen, that: even Julius Caesar would have taken heed and stayed indoors. Mind you, she encouraged me. I think that after the business of the scholarship I had become a rather tragic figure: the born genius, his hopes blighted on the bough. Anyone in that situation is a genius by common consent: there's no drama in it otherwise. Moira had faith in me: I was not to give up; talent would prevail. I was flattered: in those days I was not attractive to girls. Soap and water and I were not on intimate terms; a handkerchief was something to be purely as a decoration in one's Sunday suit. Well, the world may have been there for

the taking. I took Moira. We courted, we became engaged, we married.
Eoghain I'm not goin' to.
Owen No?
Eoghain I've nothin' against it. Maybe someday. But not till I get fixed up.
Owen You sound so incorruptible.
Eoghain Dunno. But I'll tell you one thing . . . If . . . (*He stops*)
Owen If?
Eoghain If I thought I was no good at this lark, or if I'd ever let an'thin' get
  in me way . . . if I thought that, I'd go over to the quarry cliff beyant an'
  heave meself off it. You can laugh again at me——
Owen Please.
Eoghain—but I would. So how did you . . . fix it?
Owen What?
Eoghain Get away.
Owen Oh. So we were married. Sundays were kept aside for tea with those
  parents of mine who had decided to live until they were a hundred. Within
  a month of the wedding, my father became ill. He died. My mother went
  off to live with a sister of hers in Scotland . . . quite cheerfully, *she* left *me*.
  At long last, I was free. Of them, that is; but now, instead of parents, I had
  a wife. Only then did it occur to me that responsibilities are links in a
  chain. Parents, a job with prospects, a wife, children.
Eoghain Did you have kids?
Owen Moira wanted a family. I think she was not so much a woman as a
  conceiving apparatus. In between miscarriages, she managed to find dabs
  of oil paint on the curtains and upholstery. She developed new theories on
  art and artists. A hobby, as she took to calling what I did, was best
  relegated to Sundays. Then she pointed out that a man wearing old
  clothes in our town on the sabbath and carrying paints and canvases was
  making a show of himself. "People will think you're queer," she said, not
  meaning it, of course, in the present-day colloquial sense.
Eoghain In the what?
Owen You know. Queer . . . being . . .
Eoghain Bein' what?
Owen (*staring at him*) Perhaps you *shouldn't* go abroad. No matter. In my
  innocence, it took me a while to realize that she was fighting a rival,
  fighting it to the death, blindly, as if it were a mistress. It wasn't my poor
  splashes of colour on canvas she hated—my attempts to make the muscle
  I spoke of between the brain and the pencil take a detour by way of the
  heart. It was a rival passion and she determined to destroy it. Painting was
  nice, but what *use* was it? The man next door had an allotment: *he*
  produced cabbages. Women are so energetic: men get tired and give up;
  they never do. I fought a losing war . . . and damn it, it wasn't fair! No; no
  details. You don't even have a girl-friend yet: why should I spoil what lies
  ahead? But even when I at last walked out and took passage for
  Holyhead, hers was the sincere amazement of a loving parent who has
  raised a brat.
Eoghain I bet there was holy stink.
Owen There was anger certainly.

Eoghain Did she folley you? To England.

Owen No. As soon as I could, I made financial arrangements, but I never saw her again.

Eoghain Never?

Owen She still lives not far from here.

Eoghain You're havin' me on.

Owen How?

Eoghain It's all a yarn. Just now you told me your wife went for a taxi.

Owen Ah. But a man may have more than one wife, may he not?

Eoghain I see ... You mean, you and the ... the first lady got ...

Owen Divorced? You can say the word: no-one is listening. No, we did not. My wife invoked her religious principles ... it's such a rare pleasure when they actually come in useful. No divorce ... never.

Eoghain But the lady who went for the——

Owen She is my wife. Do you understand me?

Eoghain Yeah, sure.

Owen You seem shocked.

Eoghain Me? Not at all. None of my business.

Owen Marriage and wedding have less in common than you might think.

Eoghain So what happened in England?

Owen I studied for three years. I survived, worked at this and that. My wife—the lady you would call my wife—was gleefully pressing me for arrears of maintenance, so a friend wangled me a job as an illustrator. It was for a magazine serial ... you know the sort: "Lady Elspeth, her magnificent breasts heaving with terror, shrank from the lewd gaze of the Roundhead captain". It and I were a roaring success. I did more of the same, and I came to acknowledge what I had suspected: that while I was aspiring to the more enduring kind of art, the talent was never there. The Holy Ghost had looked upon me and said: "Next"!

Eoghain You mean——

Owen Now I have my own agency. I do very little of the actual art work, it's nearly all supervision and admin.

Eoghain Then you did it all for nothin'.

Owen Pardon me?

Eoghain For nothin'. All that studyin' an' workin' and then flakin' off to England. Doin' what you did ... all o' that, and you gev up.

Owen I found out what I could do best, and I did it.

Eoghain laughs, shaking his head

You're so bloody smug. I'm happy. I'm solvent, I enjoy my work. I've done everything worth doing, and you call that nothing.

Eoghain It has shag-all to do with me.

Owen I said, you call it nothing.

Eoghain It's not what you went after.

Owen Perhaps it isn't. But do you think I'd have got as much by staying here? You're so damned untarnished just because you haven't been out in the world and had your arse kicked. Well, if you ever get up the gumption to leave this hole, you may discover that even you are less than a reincarnation of Rembrandt, Velasquez and Renoir rolled into one fat tube of paint.

Eoghain Maybe so, but I'll tell you this. I won't give up.

Owen No?

Eoghain You think I will?

Owen Probably not. If smugness and complacency are any qualifications, then you'll probably do very well. Nothing dents that self-approval, does it, my shabby friend?

Eoghain (*stung*) You just . . . feck off. An' if you won't, I will.

Owen No, that was uncalled for. I apolo——

Eoghain (*looking off*) Your . . . uh, (*with a sneer*) your wife is back.

He starts off

Owen No, wait. Stay and meet her. Come with us.

Eoghain is out of sight

Rosemary appears from the other direction

Rosemary (*breathless*) Twice in one day. And you promised you'd rest.

Owen I said I'd stay here, and I did.

Rosemary How do you feel?

Owen Fine. Back to normal.

Rosemary You're still not walking back. The hotel is sending a car, it'll be at the gates by the time we are. Are you ready?

Owen In a minute. I've had company.

Rosemary Here?

Owen (*looking*) See? There he—no, he's gone. Either he'd had enough of me, or he didn't relish the prospect of coming face to face with a scarlet woman.

Rosemary What are you talking about?

Owen That boy. A youth who was sketching the view. We talked. He was quite talented.

Rosemary Praise indeed, coming from you.

Owen Oh, yes. Talent to spare, heaps of it.

Rosemary Did you tell him so?

Owen He was a little too sure of himself, too incorruptible. The young can be so damn patronizing, they know it all. He's going to clear off to England and become a giant.

Rosemary Perhaps he will.

Owen I don't know. He may not be all there.

Rosemary How?

Owen I told him I'd had heart surgery, and he'd never heard of it. And I'd swear the moon landings and the microchip were mysteries to him as well. As for homosexuality . . .

Rosemary You seem to have covered everything. Well, they say that Ireland is a breeding ground for eccentrics.

Owen Not at his age. They take time to mature.

Rosemary Shall we go down?

Owen I talked to him as though I'd known him for years. A scarecrow. His nose needed blowing ... the sort of lad who thinks a handkerchief is purely a decoration for his Sunday—— (*He breaks off*)

Rosemary What is it?

Owen His face.

Rosemary Are you ill? It's come back hasn't it?

Owen No ...

Rosemary Then what's wrong?

Owen I know the face, that's all. I know it. I remember. Yes, now I remember.

Rosemary Where you've seen him.

Owen No ... no, not him.

Rosemary Then who? You are ill.

Owen How long ago? Thirty years ... not long after the war, I was sitting here, sketching the view. Didn't wash too frequently, not in the winter, because in our house you had to boil a kettle. I must have been quite scruffy to look at. A middle-aged man came up ... sleek, well-dressed: prosperity shone from him like a beacon. We talked. He told me about the life he'd led, what he'd done with it. I was disgusted. I thought him the most corrupt man I'd ever met.

Rosemary Owen ... ?

Owen That boy ... what's to become of him? Oh, my God, that poor boy.

He remains quite still, Rosemary looking at him, waiting

CURTAIN

Roman Fever

Adapted from the story by
Edith Wharton

CHARACTERS

Mrs Slade
Mrs Ansley
Head Waiter

ROMAN FEVER

Adapted from the story by Edith Wharton

The terrace of a restaurant in Rome. The year is 1930, the time mid-afternoon

The only furnishings are two basket-chairs and a small table

Two middle-aged American ladies enter

Mrs Slade leads the way: she is more vivacious, more forceful, than her friend, Mrs Ansley. The Head Waiter comes into view and stands apart, watching them

Mrs Slade This will do nicely. Oh, yes, it's still the most beautiful view in the world. Wouldn't you say?

Mrs Ansley It always will be, to me.

Mrs Slade (*amused*) To you?

Mrs Ansley What?

Mrs Slade Sometimes I think you have a pen in your brain. You take it and draw a line under every single word, you really do. (*She looks down at the view*) Heavenly ... and the Forum is still there. Not that I can imagine one good reason why it shouldn't be. Let's sit.

Mrs Ansley There's that head waiter ...

Mrs Slade Yes?

Mrs Ansley I think he's wondering.

Mrs Slade I'll cure him of wondering.

She signals to the Head Waiter who at once comes over

Waiter Signora?

Mrs Slade My friend and I and our daughters have so much enjoyed our luncheon. Now as old lovers of your city we would like to admire the view until the young ladies return from——

She looks enquiringly at Mrs Ansley, who looks back helplessly

From wherever they've gone. (*She takes money from her bag*) So if we're not at all in your way ...

Waiter Prego. E un pizcere. Two mos' charming ladies, please do not be disturb. And if perhaps you would honour us by remaining for dinner ...

Mrs Slade We'll see.

Waiter La Luna. Is night of full moon. Grazie.

He bows and goes

Mrs Slade Which shines only on this restaurant.

Mrs Ansley giggles

Italians!

Mrs Ansley Oh, aren't they!

Mrs Slade Well, what I say is, if you can't laugh at them, stay at home. Where *are* the girls? Do *you* know?

Mrs Ansley I think those young aviators we met at the Embassy invited them to fly to Tarquina for tea.

Mrs Slade Do you mean—and come back in the dark?

Mrs Ansley There's a——

Mrs Slade Full moon, yes. Moonlight! What a part it still plays. Do you suppose they're as sentimental as we were?

Mrs Ansley Were we? I've really come to the conclusion that I don't in the least know what they are. (*She dips into her bag and takes out her knitting*) And I'm glad of it.

Mrs Slade For pity's sake.

Mrs Ansley Pardon me?

Mrs Slade That sublime panorama at your feet, and you want to knit. Grace Ansley, I despair of you. You're so ... American.

Mrs Ansley smiles and begins knitting

Are you aware that when we first met here we were younger than the girls are now?

Mrs Ansley That was in nineteen——

Mrs Slade And do you know what has puzzled me across the years, what I find inexplicable? What puzzles me is that for two people who could not be more dissimilar we were both copycats. Shame the devil, yes, we were. We both of us got engaged here, you to Horace me to Delphin. We both went to live on East Seventy-third Street. I had Jenny, you had Barbara. And your Horace and my Delphin both passed away within months—weeks!—of each other. We did *everything* together.

Mrs Ansley You moved.

Mrs Slade I call it uncanny ... I did what?

Mrs Ansley Away from East Seventy-third Street.

Mrs Slade Well, naturally. We owed it to ourselves to move. That was after Delphin made his *coup.*

Mrs Ansley His ... ?

Mrs Slade C-o-u-p, dear. Do you know, did I tell you, that Delphin would look out across the street at your house, at number twenty-three and say: "I'd as soon live opposite a speakeasy; at least one might see it get raided."

Mrs Ansley looks mildly affronted

(*Appeasingly*) He was joshing! You know what Delphin was like ... sweet heavens, Grace, you of all people.

Mrs Ansley Of all people?

Mrs Slade Who better?

Mrs Ansley Me?

Mrs Slade (*moving to firmer ground*) I mean the likelihood of any one raiding you and Horace. That exemplary man. Policemen with axes, chopping down his respectable door.

She laughs, her amusement just too overdone. Mrs Ansley smiles politely, letting the joke run out of momentum

So, after his *coup* . . . his success, Delphin bought into upper Park Avenue. Other lawyers, failures by comparison, lived there, why not us? (*She rises, looks again at the view and frowns sulkily*) So deadly dull.

Mrs Ansley The avenue? Not Rome?

Mrs Slade Widowhood.

Mrs Ansley Ah.

Mrs Slade I don't like it. I'm not a fool, I don't smile and pretend otherwise: I do not like it. Widow . . . hood. Yes, that's what it is, a dowdy, drab, grey hood that covers you from head to toe.

Mrs Ansley That would be a cloak, I think.

She knits placidly. Mrs Slade looks at her critically

Mrs Slade So literal. Earthbound. Yes, that is you, Grace, for the world to see, tied to earth by leaden feet. No imagination, no . . . wings.

Mrs Ansley (*cheerfully*) It's true. I've never flown.

Mrs Slade So comfortable.

Mrs Ansley I wasn't always. There are times when I think I learned it from Horace. He could turn comfort into a virtue.

Mrs Slade shakes her head in mock despair and again faces the view

I do believe you're of the opinion that dull widowhood suits me because I'm dull too.

Mrs Slade Never.

Mrs Ansley shrugs, unconcerned

And don't look indifferent, don't you dare. Do you imagine I could harbour unkind thoughts of my oldest friend? For shame.

Mrs Ansley There's no unkindness: I like being dull. It's restful: people talk to you and don't expect clever words in return. I'm sure you find it more painful to be alone than I do. You were more active in the world.

Mrs Slade If you knew.

Mrs Ansley The change is greater.

Mrs Slade I lived a life where every day brought its obligations. With Delphin, how could it be otherwise? I was the kind men called (*with wry distaste*) "handsome". You were the one they flocked to.

Mrs Ansley No such thing.

Mrs Slade In your day you were exquisite. Why deny it? Nature's favourite. You were the candle, they the moths. No! . . . a lily of the field.

Mrs Ansley Was I?

Mrs Slade "Behold them, they toil not——"

Mrs Ansley I know it! ". . . neither do they spin". Me? But how dreadful.

Mrs Slade My dear, you were angelic. Why I'm surprised you didn't steal Delphin right from under my nose. How could any young man resist? Luckily for me, handsome was as handsome did.

Mrs Ansley (*confused, faintly*) Steal him indeed.

Mrs Slade (*playfully*) But bless your generosity, our friendship prevailed. Thank the stars, I always knew how to dress, that was a beginning. Otherwise I simply asked myself "What is best for Delphin?" and then it was easy. And no-one dare say that I failed to live up to him or he to me. One day I had the satisfaction of overhearing a most eminent man, a colleague of Delphin's. He said: "Is that really his wife? Slade's wife? Generally the wives of celebrities are such ... frumps." Immodest as it may sound, I don't call that an unearned compliment.

Mrs Ansley No. No, it was——

Mrs Slade And now what have I? No entertaining of clients, no unexpectedly having to rise to an occasion. I say it's dull and I do not like it. Suddenly, brutally, there's no-one to live up to, no-one to take care of.

Mrs Ansley You have Jenny.

Mrs Slade Who? Have you forgotten? Jenny takes care of *me*.

Mrs Ansley (*smiling*) Yes, so she does.

Mrs Slade She's my jewel beyond price. Could any mother ask for more?

Mrs Ansley So affectionate.

Mrs Slade Isn't she! Mind you, there are days when I wish that that paragon of devotion would fall in love.

Mrs Ansley It will come.

Mrs Slade Even with the wrong man.

Mrs Ansley Why, Alida Slade!

Mrs Slade Don't you see? Then I could spy on her, out-manœuvre her, be more clever than she is, and in the end save her from herself. Instead, it's Jenny who watches me, who keeps me out of draughts. I catch cold and she's there with my medicines. Your daughter now ... your Barbara, she would neglect me *beautifully*.

Mrs Ansley Babs? No such thing.

Mrs Slade The girl's a miracle. I've often wondered, ever so respectfully, of course, how two such unimpeachable characters as you and Horace could manage to produce a creature quite so dynamic.

Mrs Ansley Is she? I've never noticed.

Mrs Slade Mind, if I were a chronic invalid, alone and palely loitering, as Mr Keats says, I'd rather be in my Jenny's hands. But being in the bloom of health—well, I always longed for a brilliant daughter and never quite understood why I got an angel.

Mrs Ansley I look upon Babs as an angel, too.

Mrs Slade Beyond question. But she's got rainbow wings. So vivacious. And now they're wandering by the sea with their young airmen, and here we sit and——

A bell far-off, chimes the hour. Other bells join in

Four o' clock already.

Mrs Ansley How we dawdled over lunch. There's bridge at the Embassy at five.

Mrs Slade I don't think I could face bridge. Not unless you want to.

Mrs Ansley I'd much rather stay here. It's so full of old memories.

Mrs Slade Isn't it? And what different meanings Rome has for such generations of travellers. For our grandmothers, Roman fever. For our mothers, more sentimental dangers—do you remember how closely we were guarded? And for our daughters, no more danger than the middle of Main Street.

Mrs Ansley If you don't count aeroplanes.

Mrs Slade I mean another kind of danger. I've always believed that our mothers had a much more difficult job than our grandmothers. When Roman fever stalked the city it must have been easy to gather in the girls at the danger hour. But when you and I were young, with such beauty calling us and the spice of disobedience thrown in, and no worse dangers than catching cold during the cool hour after sunset, our mothers were hard put to it to be our chaperones.

Mrs Ansley (knitting) Two, three, slip. Yes, they must have been.

Mrs Slade Whenever I look at the Forum now, I remember a great-aunt of yours, wasn't she? A dreadfully wicked great-aunt.

Mrs Ansley Aunt Harriet? Do you mean her?

Mrs Slade She was supposed, wasn't she, to have sent her young sister out to the Forum to gather a——

Mrs Ansley A night-blooming flower for her album. All our great-aunts and grandmothers kept albums of dried flowers.

Mrs Slade But she really sent her because they were in love with the same man. The poor younger sister caught the fever, didn't she, and died. As your great-aunt intended.

Mrs Ansley It was a family story. My mother used to frighten us with it when we were children.

Mrs Slade And you frightened *me* with it.

Mrs Ansley When?

Mrs Slade That winter when we both came here as girls. The winter I was engaged to Delphin.

Mrs Ansley I never did.

Mrs Slade No?

Mrs Ansley I mean, of all people I could frighten ... you!

Mrs Slade You did with that story. Perhaps it was because I was too happy. Do you know what that means? I thought: there's no more Roman fever, but the Forum is deathly cold after sunset, especially after a hot day. And the Colosseum is even colder and damper.

Mrs Ansley The Colosseum?

There is a startled quality in her voice. Mrs Slade looks away from her, at the sky. A pause

Mrs Slade The sun is setting. You're not afraid, my dear?

Mrs Ansley Of darkness?

Mrs Slade Of catching cold. I remember how ill you were that winter. As a girl you had such a delicate throat.

Mrs Ansley I caught a chill.
Mrs Slade Threatened pneumonia!
Mrs Ansley (*smiling, nervously*) No ...
Mrs Slade I say yes! (*Casually*) It wasn't easy to get into the Colosseum after the gates were closed for the night. Still, in those days it could be managed. It *was* managed, often. Lovers met there who couldn't meet elsewhere. It had that reputation.
Mrs Ansley Had it? I don't recall.
Mrs Slade Don't you? You don't remember going to visit some ruins one evening, just after dark, and catching a bad chill? You were supposed to have gone to see the moon rise, and our friends afterwards said that that expedition was what caused your illness.
Mrs Ansley Did they? It was so long ago.
Mrs Slade And you got well again, so it didn't matter. Not one bit.
Mrs Ansley I daresay even the most prudent girls aren't always prudent. (*She composes herself, then gathers the nerve to ask her question*) Alida, why did you suddenly mention the Coloss—— (*She breaks off as:*)

The Head Waiter again appears. He crosses briskly and bows

Waiter Scusi. If the signore permit ... (*He switches on the table lamp*) Grazie.

The Head Waiter leaves

Mrs Slade Go on, Grace. Why did I mention ...?
Mrs Ansley No matter, really. It's not important.
Mrs Slade Nor is it. I can't think why I brought it up. (*With affection*) Because there is not a soul in the wide world of whom I have less right to think unkindly than of you.
Mrs Ansley But why ever should you?
Mrs Slade (*thinking, then shrugging helplessly*) Envy.
Mrs Ansley Of me? Envy?
Mrs Slade It's crazy.
Mrs Ansley Yes.
Mrs Slade Envy, it's insane, it's unjustified, but there it is. I don't want your life. I've had my own, and I've got quite a distance still to go—you can bet your bottom dollar on that, Grace Maxwell Ansley! I don't know, maybe I envied you once when we were young and you were so beautiful, and I never cured myself.

Mrs Ansley smiles and shakes her head

And now here I am baring my soul over *your* knitting. Why don't we order a Martini?
Mrs Ansley (*amused*) Alida!
Mrs Slade A Martini, why not? Do you think they do American drinks here?
Mrs Ansley Perhaps we should be getting back to the hotel. Barbara and Jenny promised to be in time for dinner.
Mrs Slade That pair? They're in the clouds.

Mrs Ansley Are they?
Mrs Slade Not clouds of sentiment, like we were. Real clouds—up there.
Mrs Ansley Aeroplanes! Don't.
Mrs Slade Darling, they'll be just fine. The only accident that's likely to happen——
Mrs Ansley You mustn't.
Mrs Slade —will be to the heart of that Campolieri boy, the Marchese. Your dynamic Barbara has made a conquest.

Mrs Ansley smiles

Don't look so innocent, my dear, you know she has. Babs carries all before her, so what chance does my poor Jenny have?
Mrs Ansley Poor, indeed.
Mrs Slade My ministering angel. That shrinking violet who spends her time in your girl's shadow. I think they should be kept apart: maybe then Jenny could show herself to advantage. I certainly don't want an old maid on my hands.
Mrs Ansley Alida, she's twenty.
Mrs Slade And I'm forty-three and she mothers me. To extinction. (*Almost conspiratorially*) Grace ... I have set my sights on just the ideal young man.
Mrs Ansley No!
Mrs Slade Perfect.
Mrs Ansley For Jenny?
Mrs Slade Good family ... not exactly passengers on the "Mayflower" but then who was? Harvard graduate, and now he's on Wall Street. Not an adventurous bone in his body, which will suit Jenny beautifully.
Mrs Ansley (*amused*) She's fond of him, I hope.
Mrs Slade Well, she knows she's hardly likely to marry a Marchese, who only happens to be the best match in Rome. I wouldn't be one bit surprised if he's proposed to Barbara by now.

All this has been said in bantering good humour. Mrs Ansley has stopped knitting. Now she lowers her eyes

Well, why ever not? When you think of those young people under the spell of soaring high above the earth, who can tell? Nothing's impossible. And your Babs *is* a go-getter. It still puzzles me how Horace and you—— Why are you smiling?
Mrs Ansley Was I?
Mrs Slade You still are. Was it something I——(*She breaks off. She realizes that what she had thought of as a joke is actually nothing of the kind*) He's already done it. The Campolieri boy has proposed to Barbara! Well, has he?
Mrs Ansley (*almost demurely*) Yes.
Mrs Slade Well, I'm——And of course she accepted. No need to be asked twice, as they say. And you let me make jokes about it. Well, you sly thing.

Mrs Ansley We were going to tell you this evening. That's why Barbara and
    Massimo flew to Tarquina ... to meet his parents.

Mrs Slade And my Jenny their ... accomplice.

Mrs Ansley They could hardly go alone.

Mrs Slade No. Well, who'd have thought of it? Now I really do have reason
    to envy you.

Mrs Ansley It happened so quickly ...

Mrs Slade A whirlwind romance. I freely do confess you've knocked me
    spinning. I am definitely *bouleversé*. (*It has been a shock. She attempts to
    rise to the occasion*) But where are my manners? This is such ... *good
    news*. I could not be happier for you. And for Barbara, of course ... the
    future Mrs——

Mrs Ansley Marchesa.

Mrs Slade What?

Mrs Ansley There's the title, you see.

Mrs Slade So there is.

Mrs Ansley Barbara a Marchesa ... I don't know what Horace would have
    thought. It's all so undemocratic, but I guess that's what Abroad is.

Mrs Slade They'll live here in Rome, then?

Mrs Ansley Naturally.

Mrs Slade (*at last seeing a silver lining*) How lovely for them. But my dear,
    what's to become of *you*?

Mrs Ansley Barbara's head is so full of plans ...

Mrs Slade You'll be in New York all alone, thousands of miles away ...
    sitting in that empty house on East Seventy-third Street and thinking of
    Barbara in far-off Italy. Grace, how tragically sad, and yet I know how
    nobly you'll endure it. At least, I'll always have Jenny close by——

Mrs Ansley Barbara and Massimo want me to live in Rome.

Mrs Slade Married or single, my faithful Jenny would——They have asked
    you to *what*?

Mrs Ansley They're so sweet. They want me to sell the New York house and
    settle down here.

As she prattles on, Mrs Slade stares at her, hatred welling up

    Of course if I agree—if, I say—I'd not for a moment be in their way. I'd
ask them to find me an apartment across town somewhere. And I'd never
really be starved for company: there's a regular colony of Americans, they
all go to the Embassy. It's all been so sudden ... my head's in a whirl. (*A
pause. She begins to collect her knitting*) Shouldn't we be getting back?
Alida?

Mrs Slade Yes, we should.

*As Mrs Ansley gathers up her things, the bitterness that is mounting in Mrs
Slade cannot be contained*

    Would you like to know——(*She breaks off, on the edge of the irrevocable*)

Mrs Ansley Yes.

Mrs Slade Would you care to be enlightened as to why I brought up the
    subject of the Colosseum just now? Where the cold is so deathly after
    sunset. Would you be interested?

Mrs Ansley I . . . I don't know.

Mrs Slade I mean, if you're going to settle down in Rome and live here happily ever after—as you deserve, Grace!—well, I may never see you again, so it's really now, isn't it, or not at all.

Mrs Ansley (*sensing danger*) Maybe back at the hotel . . .

Mrs Slade The hotel is crammed with tourists, let's enjoy our privacy. Here we are, old friends, old times . . . humour me.

Mrs Ansley Old times?

Mrs Slade Why I've put it off for so long I'll never know. Because you'll smile, Grace . . . you may even laugh. That dreadful chill you caught——

Mrs Ansley (*feebly*) Please.

Mrs Slade —so many years ago. It was because you went to the Colosseum. After dark, alone, on tiptoe and without a word to a living soul. (*She smiles brightly*) There, it's out at last! (*Still with apparent affection*) I've always wanted you to know that I knew.

Mrs Ansley Did I go there? I don't——

Mrs Slade Remember. Oh yes, you did. And I have another surprise for you. I even know *why* you went.

Mrs Ansley It's so unimportant. I——

Mrs Slade Oh, no. You mustn't say that. It may have been foolish . . . disloyal . . . wicked even, but it was not unimportant. You went there to meet the man I was engaged to. What's more, I can repeat every word of the letter that took you there.

Mrs Ansley has risen fearfully to her feet. Her gloves and knitting slip to the ground

You think I'm guessing? You went there to meet Delphin because of a note slipped under the door of your room.

Mrs Ansley No. Please don't.

Mrs Slade I know it by heart. Listen . . .

Mrs Ansley No!

Mrs Slade "My one darling . . . Things can't go on like this. I must see you alone. Come to the Colosseum immediately after dark tomorrow. There will be somebody to let you in. No-one whom you need fear will suspect." Perhaps you've forgotten?

Mrs Ansley No, I know it by heart, too.

Mrs Slade And the signature?

Mrs Ansley There was none.

Mrs Slade Only initials . . . "D.S" Was that it? I'm right amn't I? It was that letter that took you out after dark.

Mrs Ansley (*slowly*) Delphin told you.

Mrs Slade He never said a word. Not ever.

Mrs Ansley Then how could you have known? I burnt that letter at once.

Mrs Slade You would. And now you're wondering how on earth I knew what was in it? Isn't that so?

Mrs Ansley says nothing

Well, you're such an accomplished schemer, can't you guess? I knew what
was in that letter, my dear, because I wrote it.

Mrs Ansley You? You wrote it?

Mrs Slade Who else?

Mrs Ansley exclaims softly and sits, covering her face

And you ever so carefully destroyed it. Well, are you shocked? Horrified?

Mrs Ansley (*looking at her*) I wasn't thinking of you. I was thinking, it was
the only letter I ever had from him.

Mrs Slade And I wrote it. But I was the girl he was engaged to . . . did you
happen to remember that?

Mrs Ansley I'm not trying to excuse myself. I remembered.

Mrs Slade And still you went.

Mrs Ansley Still I went.

Mrs Slade You do understand? I saw it beginning to happen between
Delphin and you . . . the soft, sly looks, the moments of silence. Horace
Ansley was dancing attendance on you . . . stupid, moonstruck Horace.
He didn't notice . . . I did. I knew you were in love with Delphin, and I was
afraid of you, of your prettiness, your doll's face and your quiet ways.
Well, I wanted you out of the way, that's all. Just for a few weeks, just till
I was sure of him. So in a blind rage I wrote that letter.

Mrs Ansley And now you've told me because you've always gone on hating
me.

Mrs Slade Do I? I know I did then. I wanted you to fall ill. But that was all
. . . I never hoped you'd die, not for a moment, I swear.

Mrs Ansley does not respond. She picks up her knitting and gloves

You think I'm a monster?

Mrs Ansley Does it matter? It was the only letter I ever had, and you say he
didn't write it.

Mrs Slade My God, you care for him still.

Mrs Ansley I cared for that memory.

Mrs Slade Well, bravo, my dear. How beautifully you play the injured
party. May I remind you, you tried your damnedest to get him away from
me. But I fought you, and you lost and I won. That's all there is.

Mrs Ansley As you say . . . you won.

Mrs Slade (*sullenly*) I wish now I hadn't told you. I had no idea you'd take
on so . . . I thought you'd be amused, I really did. It all happened so long
ago, as you say. And it isn't as if you loved him. It was an infatuation: you
simply wanted what was mine. You were hardly over your illness when
you accepted Horace Ansley. Does that sound like love? I knew you did it
out of *pique*, to be able to say you'd got ahead of Delphin and me. Girls
have such silly reasons for doing serious things. And when you married so
soon, then I knew you never cared.

Mrs Ansley Then there's no harm done. Well, then!

She turns to go. Mrs Slade is anxious to absolve herself

Mrs Slade It needn't affect our friendship. You could say I did it as a joke.

Mrs Ansley (*stopping*) A joke?

Mrs Slade Well, girls are cruel sometimes, girls in love especially. And I remember laughing to myself all that evening. You were outside the Colosseum, dodging out of sight, listening for every sound, trying to get in. Waiting for him. I really was upset when you were so ill afterward.

Mrs Ansley Waiting? Why should I have had to wait?

Mrs Slade For Delphin!

Mrs Ansley But he was there. He'd arranged everything. We were let in at once.

Mrs Slade There? Delphin was there? Now you're lying.

Mrs Ansley He kept the appointment.

Mrs Slade What appointment? You're raving, you're insane. How could he have known?

Mrs Ansley Because I answered the letter.

Mrs Slade You——

Mrs Ansley Didn't you think I would? I wrote and told him I'd be there. So he came.

Mrs Slade Oh, my God. You answered it. I never thought . . .

Mrs Ansley No, I suppose you were too angry. You should have considered . . . after all, we were both of us taught to reply to invitations. It *is* cold here . . . we'd better go back. I'm sorry for you, Alida. Truly.

Mrs Slade For me? Sorry? How dare you!

Mrs Ansley After all, I didn't have to wait that night.

Mrs Slade Yes, I was beaten there. But I oughtn't to begrudge you your little triumph, your few minutes with Delphin. It was I who won in the end. I had him for twenty years. All you ever had was that one letter he didn't write.

Mrs Ansley is silent for a moment. They are both ready to leave

Mrs Ansley I had Barbara.

She goes out

Mrs Slade is quite still

The Head Waiter appears at the rear, ready to bow her out

As she slowly turns to go

                    the CURTAIN *falls*

Pizzazz

CHARACTERS

Marion
Olivia
Rooney
Conroy
Mrs Hand

PIZZAZZ

A reception area. Afternoon

The Royal Brosna Line is one of the companies which hire out cabin cruisers on the River Shannon. The reception area is a bright, functional room with a small desk, a sofa and chairs covered in matching patterns of green and saffron, and tables on which there are brochures and boating magazines. On the walls there are plans and elevation drawings of various types of hire craft. Most prominent is a large simplified map of the Shannon showing channels and markers. In a corner of the room the holiday baggage of two people is heaped up. There are two doors, one behind the desk, marked "Private", and another, the main entrance, alongside which runs a jetty. Mooring rings and cleats are visible along the length of the jetty

At rise of CURTAIN, *Marion is seen at the end of the jetty. She is American: middle-aged, vivacious, curious, boundlessly energetic. She is dressed in chic yachting clothes, including slacks, a blue windcheater with red lining and inflatable pockets, and a trim yachting cap. She is looking out across the lake*

There are two people in the reception area. One, behind the desk, is the Dispatcher, Fergal Rooney, a young man who radiates lack of enthusiasm for anything in sight. He is reading a newspaper, his lips moving as he does so. The other person is Olivia Gaynor. She, like Marion, is dressed in boating gear, but with less emphasis on seeming the Compleat Yachtswoman. She is in her mid-thirties, attractive, capable. She is leafing through brochures with the air of one who has unwanted time on her hands.

There is the sound of a cruiser's diesel engine. Marion waves energetically

Marion *(calling)* Hi, there ... hello. I mean, ahoy ... avast or something. *(In the manner of a New York telephonist)* Come in, Number Fi-ev, your ti-em is up!

There is no response from the crew of the unseen cruiser. The engine noise fades as the vessel moves further out

(Shrugging) So be like that, see if I care. *(Shouting)* Bon voyage, Titanic! *(She walks back to the reception area as if the jetty were a walkway for a parade of fashion models. Lilting:)*

> "A pretty girl is like a melody
> That haunts you night and day ..."

(Entering the reception area; to Olivia) It beats me. They just keep going round in circles out there as if they were looking for a body. And all the

time clockwise ... why is that? (*To Rooney*) Is it a union rule of some kind? Sir?

Rooney Pardon me?

Marion Those boats of yours ... the six boats?

Rooney Cruisers.

Marion Thank you. They keep going in a clockwise direction. If viewed from above. If you were in the lake and drowning—looking up, I mean— it would be anticlockwise. Is there a reason for that?

Rooney Don't ask me.

Marion I thought I *had* asked. (*To Olivia*) How's about it, Olly ... you want to play some more Scrabble?

Olivia No, thanks. You always win.

Marion I *play* to win. Tell you what I'll do. I'll give you the J, the X and the Z and throw in a blank. It's verbal suicide, but they don't call me Last Chance Lola for nothing. Penny a point?

Olivia Will you promise to use English spelling instead of American?

Marion Never!

Olivia Then no.

Marion (*echoing*) No. It's idiotic. "Harbour" ... h-a-r-b-o-*u*-r. Why do you people take a perfectly simple word and stick a "u" in it?

Olivia We didn't stick it in. It was already there, and you people threw it out.

Marion Americans believe in simplicity of language.

Olivia I know. Like "faucet" for "tap" and "elevator" for "lift".

Marion I could order you to play Scrabble. As my employee.

Olivia gives her a steady unintimidated look

(*Wheedling*) So how's about a little backgammon? Two-handed bridge? Five-card stud? Pinochle? Craps?

Olivia Gin rummy?

Marion You got it. (*She tears her windcheater off and finds a pack of cards in her bag. To Rooney*) Sir, do we have time for a little gin? Young sir?

Rooney (*without looking up*) I'm not here. Drink away.

Marion Pour. Make a note of that, Olly. East Galway colloquialism for to deal or distribute. Cut for drink.

They cut the cards

Mine ... oh, goody. Tell you what we're going to do to make it interesting. While we play, you tell me your life story. The works.

Olivia You got that out of me the first day I came to you. Three years ago.

Marion So give me the three years. Come on, Olly, be a pal and dish the dirt ... we could be stuck here all day.

To Rooney, who does not react

Right? Right. You think those are just boats ... cruisers out there? They are Flying Dutchmen, doomed to sail in small circles for eternity. They are never coming in. So give me a break. Who are you laying? What's his name? Is his wife pretty?

Olivia Marion, you are the most inquisitive——(*She breaks off as:*)

G. P. Conroy arrives. He is a professional man of Marion's age: Irish, probably more attractive now than when he was younger. He is dressed in well-cut casual clothes

Marion looks at him with immediate interest

Marion Whoops.
Olivia Your play. Marion?
Marion Down girl. There are more exciting things in life even than gin rummy.

Conroy stands at the desk waiting for Rooney to take notice of him. He coughs. Rooney continues to read his paper

Conroy Are you in charge here?

Rooney looks up

Marion Pardon me, but——
Conroy Do you mind? I was here first.
Marion You want to bet?
Conroy (*to Rooney*) I asked if you're the person in charge.
Rooney Yis.
Conroy Is it possible to hire a boat?
Marion (*helpfully*) A cruiser.
Conroy (*ignoring her*) I mean, today.
Rooney It might be.
Conroy Well, is it possible or isn't it?

As Rooney looks at him:

When you've quite finished counting both my heads and arrive at a total, might I have an answer?
Rooney There's industrial action.
Conroy Do you mean a strike? You're telling me that I cannot have a ... (*aware that Marion is listening*) ... a vessel?
Rooney I'm saying nothing, but ye might if ye wait.
Conroy For how long? (*Ranting*) Christ, what a country. It has precisely two of everything. One is the wrong size, and the other one is due in on Wednesday.
Marion Careful ... blood pressure.
Conroy Madam, I happen to be a doctor.
Marion Gravediggers also die.
Conroy (*to Rooney*) I asked you, for how long?
Marion He's not here.
Conroy What?

She takes his arm and leads him to the door

Marion Doc, allow me. You see those white cruisers out there? Circling? Well——

As he turns back to Rooney

No, you stick with me, it'll save time. It seems that today, all over this beautiful country of yours—and of mine by adoption—there are marches protesting against the level of unemployment. It seems that when your people complain about having no work to do, they mark the occasion by doing no work. Well, those cruisers are protesting.

Conroy (*pointing*) *That* is a protest march?

Marion Give the man a cigar.

Conroy Good God.

Marion And just as soon as they quit marching in Dublin and points west, that phone will ring and we'll get our cruisers. Until then, I guess we're all in the same——(*Catching herself in time*) Oh, boy.

Now that Conroy has his information, he walks away from her brusquely

(*Murmuring*) "Why, thank you, kind lady, for your assistance." "Think nothing of it, sir, have a nice day."

Conroy Bloody incredible. (*To Olivia*) Are you affected by this walk on water?

Olivia Afraid so. We've been waiting these two hours.

Conroy An Irish accent ... praise be. There seems to be nothing in this wilderness excepted damn Germans and (*lowering his voice*) bloody Americans. (*Glowering at Rooney*) Deplorable state of affairs. It's this sort of bolshie attitude towards visitors that's ruining the tourist industry.

Olivia (*politely*) Isn't it!

Conroy Tell me ... it's my first time for hiring one of these ... (*deliberately*) boats. Are there cooking facilities?

Olivia Oh, yes. I mugged up on it: there's a cooker on board with an oven and gas rings.

Conroy Good. Thank you.

Olivia The Shannon is such a beautiful river. And you can just meander along at your own pace.

Conroy No doubt. Well, I don't intend to meander anywhere. I'm going to be right here, attached to this quay.

Marion, listening, is keenly interested

Olivia In a cruiser?

Conroy That *is* permitted?

Olivia I assume so. But ... (*It is none of her business; she lets it go*)

Marion (*drifting past; sotto*) Ask him why.

Conroy From here I do not move.

Olivia It is a pretty spot, isn't it?

Marion throws her eyes up. Conroy is so white-hot with anger, however, that a question is unnecessary

Conroy My entire holiday is in fritters. My wife and I——

Marion Oh.

Conroy —saw a six-column-inch hotel advertisement, personal page of the *Irish Times*, no less. An oasis of calm; friendly, willing staff; all mod cons; superlative cuisine; relax and be pampered in de luxe tranquillity.

Marion (*sympathetic*) Uh-oh.

Conroy I suppose the hotel *was* an oasis, if that means a watering hole where the local animal life gathers at nightfall to drink and enshrine their patriot dead until dawn in ballad and bedlam. As for the staff, as far as willingness was concerned they were intestate. The all mod cons included a toilet that was unflushable and a hot water tap that haemorrhaged a cold viscous brown slime. As for the superlative cuisine, we should have known what lay ahead when I asked the waitress if the tomato soup was tinned and she said——

Marion Tinned?

Olivia He means canned.

Conroy If it was tinned, and she assured us that no, it was thick. After that repast, my wife has been vomiting all night, and today she is in such a demoralized condition that either we return home or go where we can do our own cooking. So here I am.

Marion You poor lambs.

Conroy It's iniquitous. To serve food in this day and age that is uneatable is——

Marion Unspeakable.

Olivia You should try one of those self-catering cottages down the way. They're supposed to be——

Marion Olly, hush up. Let's not lose him.

Olivia Lose him? Marion, you wouldn't.

Conroy Wouldn't what? (*To Olivia*) Is she with you?

Marion Olly—Miss Olivia Gaynor—is my dear friend, confidante and indispensable personal assistant.

Conroy Oh?

Olivia Marion . . . please. (*To Conroy*) Don't let her.

Marion (*to Olivia*) You're fired. (*To Conroy*) Your wife isn't here with you?

Conroy She's resting.

Marion In that place?

Conroy (*to Olivia*) I told her to eat and drink nothing until I get back, and in particular not to think about the veal because it induces retching. Oh, a fine holiday, and a finer wedding anniv—— (*He stops, too late*)

Marion Your anniversary? No!

Conroy Oh, Christ.

Marion But how lovely. And what a coincidence.

Conroy Is it?

Marion Most certainly. You're here and we're here, and it's your anniversary. Talk about a small world.

He looks at her as if she were mad. He walks away, affecting to study the wall map

Wood, tin or crystal? Or isn't it one of the specials? Whichever it is, I hope you're the kind of husband who sends flowers and says a thank-you for all the happy years. You should. Because, remember, we pass this way but once.

Conroy Please God.

Marion Amen. My own dear husband is no more. He passed over ... or dropped dead, as we say back home. He was Irish, a professional man, that's why I live here: it helps me to feel that he's not really gone, but lurking. So often he would say to me, even when sober: "Marion, we should grasp each fleeting moment. One of us, you or I, might not see tomorrow." He was really taken aback when it turned out to be him. For all his faults, George was not a chauvinist: he believed in ladies first.

Conroy Madam ...

Marion So how are you doing?

Conroy Excuse me. I don't want to talk to you or to anyone. Or to be talked to or at.

Marion Oh. You're mad at someone.

Conroy Yes.

Marion Don't be. She can't help being sick. Forgive.

Conroy goes to Olivia

Conroy Can you stop her? Can anyone?

Olivia Sorry.

Conroy (*to Rooney*) Can *you*?

Rooney What?

Marion Stop ... hold everything! Son of a gun, I've got it. (*A happy smile of discovery*) You don't like Americans.

Conroy Eh?

Marion You devil, you.

Conroy Please ... *please*? I don't know you. I'm a man on holiday who's having a terrible time. Why are you picking on me?

Marion Terrible time, huh?

Conroy Yes!

Marion So why do you let people kick you around? Quit being a fall guy. Get in there and come out with your dukes up. Give 'em the old one-two.

Conroy (*staring at her; then with quiet passion*) God, but I hate Americans.

Marion You said it ... oh, good.

Conroy (*regretting his rudeness*) I'm sorry.

Marion Don't be. Everyone hates us. They envy us our know-how. They want our efficiency, our pizzazz, our orthodontists, our telephones that work and our get-up-and-go. What they don't want is *us*. Why is that?

A pause

Conroy Deep down——

Marion Shoot.

Conroy —and speaking for myself, what I abominate most of all is the pizzazz.

Marion You're kidding.

Conroy Truly. I don't mind the crassness or the vulgarity. Let's be fair: if we want to feel superior to Americans, that's the price we pay. No, what

infests my brain with a desire to mutilate and maim is that blind,
boundless energy of yours, that disgusting good humour that never lets
up. Do you know what I'm saying? You have no seasons: with you, all the
year round everything's coming up bloody roses. You're the voice in the
back of the bus that wants a sing-song, the silver lining without a cloud in
sight, the tee-totaller on somebody else's morning after. You can't or
won't understand that the rest of us need unhappiness and to have our
lives go wrong: it's either that or the curse of perpetual sunshine. You're a
walking Florida. You've taken a vow of perpetual motion, and we're your
converts. Damn the lot of you: it's all sock-it-to-'em and wake-up-and-
live. You'd organize a barbecue at a cremation. (*He pauses, exhausted by
his outburst*)

Marion Attaboy. Now don't you feel terrific?

Conroy What?

Marion I always say, letting it all hang out is good for what ails you.

Conroy (*to Olivia*) Are you really her secretary?

Olivia 'Fraid so.

Conroy It's just that I saw a play once about three people locked in a room
who were dead but didn't know they were dead. And they were in Hell,
and each one was the other's tormentor. Do you think that's a possibility?

Marion Aren't you curious to know what it is I do that I should have a
secretary?

Conroy No.

Marion You're determined to worm it out of me, aren't you?

Olivia The gentleman isn't interested.

Marion What does it mean to you when I say (*coyly*) "Mainly Marion"?

Conroy Robin Hood?

Marion Oh, boy.

Olivia Marion writes a column.

Marion Olly writes a column: all I do is kick a few thoughts around.
Cracker-barrel stuff. Just for a hobby, but it's syndicated. I get fan mail.

Olivia A letter a week.

Marion When I remember to write it. It was a kind of therapy I took up
when George handed in his dinner-pail.

Conroy (*apprehensive*) You write a gossip column.

Marion Naw. I put a little zip into people's lives. You know, like the song
says: "Get up, get out, and meet the sun half-way."

Conroy I might have known. Well, I happen to believe that people can help
themselves without self-help.

Marion You do, huh?

Conroy Now, if you'll excuse me . . . (*He brushes past her*)

Marion Something else I did when George took that deep breath and forgot
to exhale was, I went back to college.

Conroy Interesting. (*To Rooney*) Excuse me, where is the nearest pub?

Marion I said to myself: There's a new life out there and it's up for grabs.
Go get it, girl.

Conroy I said, can you direct me to the nearest public house.

Rooney It's . . . uh, if you cross the bridge and turn left at the——

He sees that Marion has taken a pound note from her pocket and is shaking her head at him meaningfully

Rooney There isn't one.
Conroy Are you mad?
Rooney The owner died.
Conroy Well, where's the next nearest?
Rooney There isn't one.

Conroy stomps away in disbelief. Following him, Marion gives the pound to Rooney

Marion Bless you for that, he's an alcoholic. (*To Conroy*) I went back to college at the age of never-you-mind, and I majored in psycho-drama. You're a doctor. Don't you find psycho-drama invaluable in the areas of diagnosis and treatment?
Conroy Not often. I'm a proctologist.
Marion Oh. You mean you treat disorders of the——
Conroy Yes. And allow me to tell you that you are the most acute pain in that part of the anatomy that I have ever encountered.
Marion That's rude, but I forgive you. In psycho-drama, disturbed people act out their most intimate problems. It's a striptease of the human soul.

As Conroy starts out, she interposes herself

You don't want to go out there: you'll catch cold.
Conroy There won't be time: I'm going to throw myself in the lake.
Marion When a person acts out his inner tensions, he releases his hostilities——
Conroy Excuse me. (*He tries to pass*)
Marion —the results can be a knock out. I have seen human lives transformed. I have seen marriages saved.
Conroy Allow me. (*He gently moves her to one side and starts out*)
Marion It could even save your marriage.

Conroy walks a few paces, then stops. He returns

Conroy What did you say?
Marion I said it could. No guarantees.
Conroy (*to Rooney*) She's insane, isn't she?
Rooney 'Tis the gin.
Conroy Ah?
Rooney They've been at it all day.
Marion I bet you're one of those people who think their marriage is in pretty good shape.
Conroy No, I don't. Being Irish and not American, I treat my marriage with decency. I don't think about it at all: I ignore it.
Marion Your wife is sick, isn't she?
Conroy What of it? That was rancid veal.
Marion Uh-huh. And on your anniversary.
Conroy Well?

Marion You really don't see the significance?
Conroy (*with elaborate sarcasm*) But of course! Her vomiting is psychosomatic. It is actually a cry for help and a symptom of her aversion towards me. Now you listen. I am waiting for a boat.

As Marion opens her mouth to correct him:

Rooney Cruiser.
Marion Thank you.
Conroy I don't know you. Nonetheless, you have seen fit to accost, annoy and persecute me, and now, it seems, you want to pry into my private life. I pay my bills, I am eminent in my profession, and I've been contentedly married for twenty-five years . . .
Marion A silver wedding, I knew it.
Conroy We're total strangers, and in your case "strange" is an understatement. Why are you picking on me?
Marion Easy. You're the only game in town.

He looks at her, unwilling to comprehend. A pause

Olivia Marion is addicted to games.
Marion Any time, any place.
Olivia Two flies going up a window.
Conroy I happen to think games are for idiots. And I never gamble.
Marion No? I'll lay you five to one you've got a mole under your left armpit.
Conroy (*at once*) You lose!

She smirks. He scowls bad-temperedly

Marion Oh, come on, we have time to kill. How's about it?
Olivia (*to Conroy*) Don't play.
Conroy I won't. (*Then*) Play what?
Marion Happy Families. Or otherwise.
Conroy You *are* mad.
Marion Let me put it like this . . .
Conroy (*to Olivia*) You're really her keeper.
Marion This re-enactment of a marriage on the rocks could change your life. A scientific experiment, no horsing around. And if you won't buy that, let's say it's a load of baloney and we'll kid the hell out of it.
Conroy Certifiable.
Marion Now . . . you'll be you, of course, and I'll be——I don't think I know your wife's name.
Conroy Her name? You know *nothing* about her.
Marion I don't have to. All women are basically alike: noble, affectionate and married to bums. I could go overboard, but I want to stay impartial.
Conroy Oh, good.
Marion So . . . ! You are you, I am Mrs You, and Olly is the other woman.
Conroy *What* other woman?
Marion As well as our supporting cast.

Conroy Damn your eyes, you meddlesome bag, I've never looked at another woman.

Marion Maybe we could use a bit player as well. (*She eyes Rooney speculatively*) No, I guess not.

Rooney (*suddenly*) Last year I was——(*He stops, shy*)

Marion Pardon me.

Rooney When St Kilda's Players put on *The Vice of a Fenian*, I was the English captain.

Marion I'll be damned, a star is born.

Rooney (*still in his rural accent*) "Rebel scum, you dare to bandy words with a kinsman of the Queen?"

Marion I love it, don't change a thing. What was the Fenian's vice, by the way?

Rooney (*simply*) The vice he talked with.

Marion Oh. Forgive me, I get these black-outs. (*To Conroy*) Ready for Curtain Up?

Conroy You're up to something. You know me, don't you, or you know of me?

Marion (*candidly*) Nope.

Conroy (*turning to Rooney*) You. These are business premises, and I'm a customer. Are you going to permit this lunacy or are you going to act?

Marion He's going to act.

Conroy God in heaven.

Olivia (*to Conroy*) Excuse me, but why the fuss? A game needs players, doesn't it?

Marion (*warningly*) Olly ...

Olivia As long as you stay out of it and say nothing, what can she do?

Marion Thanks, pal.

Conroy You're right ... thank you. (*To Marion, now good-humouredly*) You carry on. Play your game, and I'll sit here and watch you make more of a fool of yourself than you already are. I'll even give you a start. My name is G. P. Conroy. I specialize in medicine because I got tired of jokes about the G.P. I interned in Minneapolis, at the Mayo Clinic. I have a wife and two children: one daughter, one grown-up son.

Rooney (*softly*) That'll be me.

Conroy Now put up or shut up.

He settles back comfortably, sure of himself. She looks at him with dislike. Then, without a change of expression:

Marion G.P., huh? What does the "G" stand for?

He shakes his head smiling

Gerald? Gareth? I think I'll call you George: it makes me feel all warm and connubial again, even though you aren't one teeny bit like him.

She moves a small table up to the chair on which Conroy is sitting, then, during the following carries a chair over so that it is facing him across the table. Conroy picks up a brochure and affects to study it

For one thing, he dressed better than you do. No offence, George, but you look like a proctologist on vacation. You aren't the anonymous sort, you know what I mean? What you'd really like is to wear your striped pants and white smock to let 'em all know you're you. I can understand your security. In your job, everybody bows to you, except that they do it in the wrong direction. But I mustn't be mean. I love you, and here it is, our fifth anniversary, (*sitting*) and you've brought me to this lovely restaurant.

Conroy blinks and looks about him

Waitress!

Olivia comes forward

Marion Waitress, my husband and I are five years married this very day. We want everything to be perfect.
Olivia We'll do our best, madam.

Conroy stares at her

Are you and the gentleman ready to order?
Marion (*glancing at a brochure*) Why not? I think that seeing as how the occasion is so meaningful, I'll start with the oysters. (*She bats her eyes at Conroy*) Then the Châteaubriand, medium rare and rarin' to go.
Olivia Thank you. And for the gentleman?
Marion George, darling?

No response

He'll have exactly the same, except double up on the oysters. (*She looks at another brochure*) And for wine the Château-Latour seventy-nine.
Olivia Thank you. *Bon appetit.*
Marion You're welcome. (*To Conroy*) Five golden years . . . here's looking at you, kid.
Conroy I'm not five years married, I'm——
Olivia (*warning him*) Ah!
Marion Twenty-five . . . I know. This is a guided tour down Memory Lane. Yes, five happy gold-plated years. Do you remember the first meal I cooked for you, George? Or didn't cook . . . I got so excited that I forgot to light the oven. You were so sweet about it. You didn't utter one reproachful word, just looked at that raw leg of lamb and walked out of the house. I wonder why brides cry so much. Maybe it's for the same reason that babies cry: it strengthens their lungs for after. You've got to admit it, George, I do have strong lungs.

He pays her no attention. She bellows

GEORGE!

He looks up, startled

We're communicating, oh good. I shouldn't have let your impatience get to me, because that was a quality of yours I liked. You were in a hurry. And angry . . . you still are. You drive home from the clinic every day in the Mercedes, you put on those Gucci slippers you wouldn't be parted from, you pour yourself a Scotch, open a bottle of French wine for later on, check your Rolex, turn on the Sony, watch the BBC news and tell me what a mess Ireland is in.

As he scowls

Honey, it's a put-on, I'm kidding. You listening to me, sourpuss? You work too hard. It can't be for the money . . . it all goes to the Internal Revenue, except when your patients pay you in cash.

He says nothing

Do you think it's possible that in five years we have exhausted all our topics of conversation?

Conroy (*quietly*) You talked him to death, didn't you?

Olivia shakes her head despairingly

Marion Who?
Conroy George.
Olivia (*signalling*) Dr Conroy . . .
Conroy (*To Olivia*) Excuse me. (*To Marion*) You pizzazzed the poor bugger into the next world, didn't you?
Marion No such thing. George was a born listener.
Conroy I can see him now, coming home, opening his newspaper and wondering if today's the day he gets beyond Mutt and Jeff.

During this, Olivia goes to Rooney and whispers to him urgently

"George, why don't you ever talk to me, George? Do you know what I did today, George? I had the girls in for coffee, George, and I read *Anna Karenina*, landscaped the garden, wall-papered the living room and turned the attic into a padded cell. Don't you think that's cute, George?"

Rooney has come over and is hovering

What do *you* want?
Rooney I'm the waiter, and I've brung the oysters.
Conroy (*snarling*) Piss off.

As Rooney retreats:

(*To Marion*) Now I bet *he* had a girl-friend.
Marion Who?
Conroy Yes, I can see her, too . . . clear as day. No oil painting, couldn't boil an egg or darn a sock, but she was the woman of his dreams. A deaf mute.
Marion (*staying calm*) That's one quality I've never gotten used to in you, George: that destructive Irish sense of humour. In the five years of our togetherness——
Conroy I am not playing this game . . .
Marion (*fondly*) Eat your oysters. (*Resuming*) I have noticed that you reserve the most cruel of jokes for those you hold dearest. I heard you,

George. We were at a party, and I was leaving early, and I called you. I said "I'm off now!" and I heard you say, corner of your mouth, to the man next to you: "She's been off for years".

Conroy Did he say that?

Marion Yes, George, you did. It was a cheap shot, not worthy of you, but that wasn't what got to me. The hell with it, any Irishman with a drink in his gut and another in his hand would set fire to his mother if it brought him a laugh. No, what riled me was your contempt.

Conroy Contempt for you?

Marion No, honey-bun: for you. You people are so screwed up, you know that? To hear you tell it, Americans are a bunch of hicks, every Englishman is a no-chin punk, and the others don't count. You're the only real salt of the earth. So bully for you. Except that I've got a hunch that underneath all those flag-waving ego trips you don't go a bundle on yourselves. I mean, you don't like you, George.

Conroy I curse the day Freud was born.

Marion If somebody takes a shine to you, you can't for the life of you see why. And if somebody loves you ... why that's so downright perverted that you pin their ears back for being a jerk. That was why you said "She's been off for years", wasn't it, George? To pin my ears back.

Conroy Balls, if you'll pardon me.

Marion I'll pardon you, but it's true. I swear it on a stack of——

Conroy "Reader's Digests."

Marion I wouldn't have brought it up on this ... (*she strokes his hand tenderly*) ... magical evening of ours, but what got under my skin was that smart-ass remark of yours about a deaf mute. Shame on you. When it came to other women, you had taste, George ... don't knock it. Leastways, I always approved of Eleanor.

She looks affectionately towards Olivia. Conroy follows her glance, as does the now avidly interested Rooney

Nice kid.

Conroy Who is? I'm getting confused. Are you talking about my marriage or yours?

Marion (*a shrug in her voice*) Choose your partner.

Conroy What?

Marion Let's call it ours. Did you have fun, George, these past five years?

Conroy (*indicating Olivia*) What about Eleanor?

Marion Later. What was it like starting out? Was the world all new and cool like lavender sheets?

Conroy opens his mouth to reply, but clams up. Marion senses that she is making progress

Hold it. (*To Rooney*) Waiter ... you can serve the wine now.

Rooney looks to Olivia for encouragement. He picks up a small flower-vase from his desk and comes forward, wary of Conroy

(*To Conroy*) In a minute you can open the conversational floodgates. (*To Rooney*) And there *you* are. That *is* the Château seventy-nine. (*She affects to inspect the label*) Attaboy ... anchors aweigh!

She watches as Rooney picks up an imaginary glass and pours from the vase, his elbows rising

(*To Conroy*) I ordered this claret because it's your——(*To Rooney*) Pardon me, I guess you're new around here. First, you pour just that teeny bit ... for tasting?
Rooney Sorry.
Marion Think nothing of it.

Rooney pours some of the wine back into the bottle, then himself tastes what is left

Rooney It's grand.
Marion Terrific. (*To Conroy*) Do you get the impression that this place is going downhill?
Rooney (*carried away; a hearty, unconvincing stage laugh*) Ah, sure it won't poison ye.
Marion I think we've created a Frankenstein. (*To Rooney*) You can leave the vase.

Rooney goes back to his desk, walking like Karloff's monster. Marion lifts an imaginary glass

Here's to us, George.
Conroy I wish this place *was* a restaurant.
Marion Why? Are you hungry?
Conroy The last meal I had was——(*He breaks off, too proud to unbend*)
Marion But of course. That appalling dinner at the O'Borgias. Olly ...

Olivia understands. She at once goes to where the cruise luggage is piled. She opens a hamper and through the following finds a paper plate, a serviette and sandwiches wrapped in cellophane

Conroy Now what?
Marion Never you mind. Why, you poor lamb, no wonder you haven't been the life of the party. You're starving.
Conroy I'll survive.
Marion My God, I can hear it. That rumbling ... your stomach is like a bowling alley.
Conroy It is nothing of the——
Marion You should have had breakfast. There is no risk factor in bacon and eggs. Every Irish hotel ought to have a sign up: "It is safe to eat the breakfasts". Olly?
Olivia Right here. (*She places the sandwiches in front of Conroy*)
Conroy What's all this?
Olivia Your Châteaubriand, sir. Medium rare.
Conroy What? Now look here ...
Marion They were for the boat.

Conroy The cruiser?
Marion The ship. Don't worry about it, if we need more I've got the makings.
Conroy I couldn't possibly. Are you sure?
Marion Virginia ham and home-made preserves. This isn't just a pretty face, you know.
Conroy (*lusting*) If you're positive ...
Marion Enjoy!
Conroy I'm starving ... thank you.

Marion crooks a finger at Olivia, who is already pouring coffee from a thermos. Conroy attacks the sandwiches with a delight that is almost tearful. One can see his defences crumbling

Marion Forgive me if I stare, but seeing a man enjoy his food always gets a woman where she lives. It's like watching Easter bunnies or the birth of a calf.

Conroy, his mouth already full, pushes the plate at her and emits an incoherent sound of encouragement, not unlike "Uhnnf"

No thank you, George, I already ate. You were going to tell me about our first five years. Look ... (*She rises, goes to the large relief map of the Shannon and indicates the spot where the river, flowing south, becomes Lough Derg*) This is where we are, right here and now, with that lake out there ahead of us. It's no rain puddle, that's for sure ... you could get shipwrecked. All those deadly shoals, lying in wait.
Rooney Not at all ... you just follow the markers.
Marion Follow the markers! What symbolism ... why, you're a poet without——
Rooney Otherwise, ye'll tear the arse out of her.
Marion Without knowing it. (*To Conroy*) Our river, yours and mine. And up here is where we started out all these years ago. (*She indicates Lough Key in the extreme north*) How far would we have come in the first five of those years, do you think? (*Pointing to a spot on the map*) This far?
Rooney Them's the Inner Lakes ... very flat country.
Marion *Was* it flat, George? In the beginning.
Conroy You're so damned curious, I'll ... (*swallowing*) ... excuse me, I'll tell you.
Marion (*happily*) You will?
Conroy Why not? The time I interned at the Mayo, they told me I had a talent for obstetrics. So I thought I'd specialize, come back home, put in my seven years. The joke was, the country had changed. Instead of having families of six or eight, the Irish were now having two or three of them and a motor car. Well, when women are no longer in labour——
Marion Neither are the obstetricians.
Conroy Right. There were other changes. According to statistics, the Irish were drinking more wines and spirits. Now wine, as you may know, when taken to excess, is conducive to haemorrhoids. So I switched to proctology.

Marion Clever!
Conroy From obstetrics.
Marion Near enough.
Conroy Excuse the subject while I'm eating.
Marion Don't mention it.
Conroy And my wife——

Olivia puts coffee in front of him

Oh, thanks.
Marion (*annoyed by the interruption*) Olly ... ! (*To Conroy*) Your wife?
Conroy (*still eating*) These are good. We weren't long married. I was still a
house man at the Richmond, long hours and short pay ... so she helped
me. She had a few bob.
Marion A few bob?
Olivia (*explaining*) *You* would say that she was loaded.
Conroy No, no. She'd had a good job ... managed to put a bit by. She
encouraged me. It was a heavy responsibility, because when a woman like
my wife is fond of a man, he is *ipso facto* a genius, otherwise it's a
reflection on her good taste. I shouldn't have said that.
Marion She's not here, George. *I'm* here.
Conroy What was it you asked? Was the world all new then, and cool? I
don't know ... I was too scared to notice.
Marion Scared?
Conroy Of being no good. Of making mistakes. I couldn't talk to a patient.
Marion *You*?
Conroy What I mean is, I couldn't talk dishonestly: I had to learn. Now I'm
the best there is. Watch. (*He goes to Olivia, his manner brimming with
charm. He takes her hand*) My dear young woman, you are a flawless
example of womanhood and almost a waste of my valuable time. Alas,
Mother Nature—may I call you Dympna?—Mother Nature, Dympna, is
forever jealous of perfection. She afflicts only the loveliest, and that is why
you and I are destined to be friends. Yes?
Olivia (*demurely*) Yes, Doctor.
Conroy So be off home with you, have nothing to eat, and be back here at
seven sharp with two of your prettiest nighties.
Olivia (*tremulous*) Hospital ... oh, no.
Conroy Think of it as a holiday ... five days of carefree idleness away from
it all.
Olivia But, Doctor ...
Conroy I must see you again. Go now ... trust me.

*With his arm about her waist, he has been leading her towards an imaginary
door*

Olivia But I can't ... I——
Conroy Do you like the theatre?
Olivia Well, yes ...
Conroy We'll go, together.

He ushers her through the "door", closes it behind her and turns to Marion

Well?

Marion Why, George, you're an old smoothie.

Conroy Not at all. You should see Technique Number Two. Excuse me. *(He picks up another sandwich, then turns on Rooney, barking at him)* Young man!

Rooney jumps to his feet, startled

Look at you. Look at that stoop, that complexion, look at those eyes. Your sort will just not be told, will you? Why do you waste my time?

Rooney *(petrified, not acting)* I don't know.

Conroy *Don't know?*

Rooney ... Sir.

Conroy *(walking around him)* What a specimen. People tell bad jokes about the Irish, do you know that? They make us out to be stupid and slow-witted. Well, so we damn well are. It's the truth, and would you care to be told why?

Rooney *(shaking)* Yessir.

Conroy We're a race of thicks, because for generations we've been starving not only our bodies but our brains with a diet of carbohydrates. Potatoes and bread, bread and potatoes. And you still haven't changed your ways, except that you now eat pesticides and additives as well. Without protein, have you any idea of what your brain *looks like*? Eeugh! Dear God, it's a wonder you're still alive. My nurse will give you a diet sheet and a prescription for the suppositories, and I don't want to see you in here again. Now get out.

Rooney Yessir. *(He flees from the room and out on to the jetty)*

Conroy Well?

Marion That was cruel.

Conroy Yes, but it was accurate. And it works.

Rooney *(looking about him)* Where's the nurse? *(He starts to take his own pulse, then reality dawns)*

Conroy Twenty years ago, I couldn't have done that. I hemmed and hawed. They wanted God ... any god, angry or merciful. Instead, I gave them a mendicant monk. How can you be Almighty God when your wife is paying the rent?

Rooney marches back in angrily

Rooney Making a fool out of a man! *(He resumes his place at the desk, snatching up his newspaper)*

Conroy And on our anniversary there wasn't a restaurant or Château-briand or ... *(picking up the vase)* ... whatever the year was. We were in a basement flat in Palmerston Park, and we had a row. *(Then)* *I* had a row.

Marion I wouldn't fight with you?

Conroy *She* wouldn't.

Marion That's dirty.

Conroy Right! I told her ... *(He hesitates)*

Marion Say it.

Conroy I said: I'm jacking it in.

Marion Are you, George?

Conroy You heard me. I'm overworked. All I am is a dogsbody in that place, and even so, I'm no damn good at it. So I'm getting out. Done, over with.

Marion Well, maybe you should.

Conroy What?

Marion Get out. Quit.

Conroy That's it, that's what she said! She had the nerve to agree with me.

Marion If you're unhappy . . .

Conroy I'm too miserable to be unhappy. I work twelve hours at a stretch, and when I get home it's textbooks until my brain is seized up. I have no life . . . where will it end?

Marion If you get to be a specialist, I should say on a golf course.

Conroy Is that meant to be funny?

Marion I just want what you want.

Conroy I'm telling you I'm exhausted. I get five hours sleep a night, and I'm fed up of being kept by you.

Marion (*a smile*) Is this my anniversary present, George?

Conroy That money was your savings, your nest egg. You're pouring it down the drain.

Marion (*shrugging*) It's my omelette.

Conroy I have three more years to go. Let's say there's a miracle and I come out the other end. Then what? I'll be a brain-damaged proctologist without even the price of a light bulb for his proctoscope. How do I begin?

Marion Others do.

Conroy Oh, sure. The charmed circle who have money and pull, and the con-men who wouldn't know a cyst from a sunburn. Or else they marry a woman whose father is an eminent quack, too old or too sick to practise. What chance do *I* have?

Marion You tell me.

Conroy I'm asking if you think I should bale out.

Marion Yes, I do. I love you, George, but not enough to put my father through medical school.

Conroy Fine. That's it, then.

Marion You hungry? I'll fix dinner. He had a hard enough time learning to play the oboe.

Conroy That is finally . . . it.

Marion affects to be busily cooking a meal. She mimes tying on her apron, breaking eggs, beating them

Marion I never understood my father.

Conroy The problem is . . .

Marion Even on her death-bed, my mother didn't ask him about other women. She said: "Gilbert, why the oboe?"

Conroy I say, the problem is——

Marion I'm listening, hon.
Conroy She ... ah called me "dear".
Marion Who? Oh. Listening, dear.
Conroy What do I do now?
Marion Do?
Conroy With my life.
Marion Well, now that we've talked it over and you've been sweet enough
to make me part of your decision, why not start up a nice family practice?
We've got money enough for that.
Conroy (*heavily*) Where have you decided on?
Marion Maybe some place where you can use what you've already learnt.
No sense in letting four years be a total write-off. What about one of those
cute villages in the west where people sit around a lot on stone walls?

He looks at her, glowering

Conroy You have it all cut and dried, haven't you?
Marion Just quick on my feet, George.
Conroy I mean, you were easily convinced.
Marion Was I?
Conroy I didn't have to twist your arm.
Marion You're the head of the family, dear. I have faith in your lack of
confidence.
Conroy (*getting steamed up*) You have, huh?
Marion Yep. Hey, we have spinach. What do you say to eggs Florentine?
Conroy I say, shag your eggs Florentine.
Marion Is that the way you like them?
Conroy I'm on to you.
Marion Are you, George?
Conroy If you want to crook me round your finger, try getting up early.
You gave yourself away then, didn't you? Didn't you?
Marion How do you shag eggs?
Conroy (*triumphantly*) You forgot to put on an act. You forgot to say:
"Don't give up, pet ... I know you can do it"! Privately, you *want* me to
pack it in, because you don't think I've got the brains and you don't think
I've got the guts.
Marion There's no fooling you, George.
Conroy I'm no idiot.
Marion But, darling, forgive me ... you did display a certain lack of faith in
yourself. You said you were no good.
Conroy That was modesty.
Marion Was it?
Conroy I set a trap for you. (*Seizing on the inspiration*) That was it, a trap.
And you walked right into it.
Marion I agreed with you!
Conroy Exactly ... disloyalty. Well, now that our marriage is exposed as a
mockery, do you know what I'm going to do?
Marion Have dinner?
Conroy Keep your dinner. I'm going to the Richmond, to help in Casualty.

And I'll qualify, just to spite you. And not as a consultant ... I'll set myself up in private practice, and in Fitzwilliam Square!

Marion (*suppressing a smile*) You wouldn't.

Conroy That swept the ground from under you. You're not burying me in some Connemara kip. Good-night!

Marion George, your shagged eggs ...

He walks out of the playlet as if from a room. He stands, simmering down. Marion returns to the here and now and approaches him

That was pretty fancy footwork.

Conroy What was?

Marion You got my number, George. You put it to me in writing.

Conroy Did I?

Marion If that's really how it was.

Conroy Near enough. You see, if a man's wife is afraid to take a chance in life, it's up to him to be strong for them both.

Marion Absolutely.

Conroy Except I think I may have got a bit carried away.

Marion You were sensational. Tell him, Olly.

Olivia I was spellbound.

Conroy Honest?

Olivia Riveted.

Conroy (*fatuously pleased*) Come off it. Mind you, I do have a natural flair for words.

Marion Listen to me. I've been through this game with a paranoid schizophrenic, and you were *better*.

Conroy Was I?

Marion (*to Rooney*) Tell him.

Rooney (*still sulking*) I'm not playing.

Conroy Begrudger.

Marion And you licked me. You won.

Conroy Ha-ha.

Marion You monster, you.

Conroy No, no. I'm ashamed. My wife is the best woman in the world. Tales out of school ... I was unchivalrous.

Marion She was weak, George. What woman isn't?

Conroy True.

Marion So where does snitching come into it? And when you qualfied and were a success, was she disappointed?

Conroy No, she seemed to have gotten over it.

Marion You see? You made her strong.

Conroy (*wanting to believe it*) No!

Marion Yes, you did, too. Hey, you want to play some more?

Conroy What? No, thank you.

Marion It'll make you feel good.

Conroy I feel superb.

Marion Quitting while you're ahead, huh?

Conroy I've already played.

Marion You just got your feet wet.
Conroy Look. You pestered me and you persecuted me, so I humoured you and I won, and that's it. Thank you for the sandwiches and the coffee. Much obliged, but I have a book I'm reading outside in the car, so if you don't——

He breaks off. Her face is contorted with grief. She emits a great convulsive sob

What is it?

She opens her mouth, but no words come, just gasps

What's up? What are you crying for?

She points a finger at him, her mouth still opening and shutting

(*To Olivia*) Good God, is this because I won't play with her?
Marion (*sobbing*) Errghh . . . errghh . . .
Conroy Get a grip on yourself. How can you be so——

He is about to say "childish" but she covers her mouth with her hand, goes to where her luggage and Olivia's is stacked and begins pulling bags this way and that

What are you doing?
Marion I'm . . . leaving.
Conroy Why? What for?

She picks up an overnight bag

All this, because you want your own way and can't have it.

As she starts towards the door:

And there's nothing out there. The boats haven't come in yet.

She turns and fixes him with a long penetrating look filled with bitterness

(*Wilting*) I mean the cruisers.
Marion I'm leaving *you*, George.
Conroy Pardon?
Marion And I'm taking the children.
Conroy Oh, for God's sake!
Marion Swear at me all you want . . . I'm through. Do you know what day today is? Our fifteenth anniversary.
Conroy Let me out of here.

He makes for the door, but she is there ahead of him, barring the way, her eyes blazing

Marion Oh no, George, I'm the one who's leaving. I've had fifteen years of you, and now it's over . . . *finito*, because I don't like you any more. I've tried. Heaven will bear witness that I've tried. I've bruised the knuckles of my heart on you.
Conroy Just get out of my——(*Then*) The what of your *what*?

Marion You needn't worry, I don't want anything from you. You can keep the house . . . I'll send for the furniture. In the meantime, Mother will find room for us.

Conroy (*suddenly smiling*) My dear woman, it won't work. This is one game you can play all on your——(*A thought occurs*) Wait a minute. Gotcha!

Marion Pardon me?

Conroy And you can't even play it properly. So you're going home to mother! Your mother is dead. You said so.

Marion Did I?

Conroy (*gloating, childlike*) Yah! Now who's clever-clogs?

Marion It so happens, George——

Conroy Breach of the rules . . . I win!

Marion It so happens that it's *your* mother we're going home to.

Conroy Eh?

Marion You know she never liked you.

Conroy Well, you lying——

Marion Which is a gross understatement on account of I have no wish to hurt your feelings.

Conroy You slanderous rip, my mother idolized me. She——

Mrs Hand enters at the point by the door marked "Private". She wears a pinafore on which is the company logo and carries a pile of bed-linen and towels. She is middle-aged, maternal, quick to sympathize

Her entrance is so unexpected that Marion, Conroy and Olivia stare at her

Mrs Hand Fergal, have they come in yet?

Rooney (*engrossed in the drama*) What? No.

Mrs Hand (*dismayed*) You're not in earnest, say they have. (*To the others*) Excuse me. (*To Rooney, lowering her voice*) I won't see my bed tonight. I have six change-overs to do, and there's a towel and a pillow-slip missing off the "Lady of Killaloe" and a teapot broke on the "Lady of Meelick". Be a good boy and call them in.

Rooney Can't.

Mrs Hand Tell them the march is over . . . yes, you will. (*Seeing that Marion is looking at her*) Isn't it very changeable?

Marion Sure is.

Mrs Hand I'm the housekeeper. We'll have you snug as bugs in rugs the minute they come in. Any second now. (*Again in a low voice*) Fergal, the people are waiting.

Rooney Let them.

Mrs Hand You're like the rest of them: you can't wait to be promoted to the dole. (*Making for a chair*) I'm staying here. 'Tis freezing inside in that hot press. (*She sinks into a chair with the glad sigh of one who has been a long time on her feet*)

Conroy (*to Marion*) Well, that's put paid to you and your game.

Marion Has it?

Olivia He's right, Marion. Call it a day.

Marion looks at both of them, then goes purposefully over to Mrs Hand

Marion Mom . . .
Olivia Marion, no.
Mrs Hand (*pleasantly*) Yes, dear, can I help you?
Marion I don't know how to tell you this——
Mrs Hand (*already sympathetic*) Oh?
Marion —because it's going to come as a terrible shock. The fact is, I'm leaving George.
Conroy (*clutching his head*) Oh, God.

Mrs Hand does not react. She looks at Marion, her face utterly devoid of expression

Marion I'm leaving him for good because my life is meaningless. And please . . . don't talk. Hear my side of it. Don't condemn me, not just yet.
Rooney Mrs Hand, ma'am . . .

Mrs Hand, without otherwise moving or acknowledging his presence, raises a hand, bidding him to silence. Conroy looks on with a horrified fascination

Marion (*on one knee, humbly*) Thank you. Forgive me for laying it on you like this, but there's no-one else I can turn to. You're so kind and sympathetic. (*She places the other woman's hand to her own cheek, squinting as she does so at the ring on the wedding finger*) You are a good warm person, and above all else . . . (*taking a chance*) . . . you are a *mother*.
Mrs Hand Am I!
Marion (*anxiously*) Are you?
Mrs Hand Don't talk to me.
Marion (*fondly*) Mom!
Mrs Hand I'd five of them.
Marion Five . . . how wonderful. (*She looks with sly malice at Conroy*) And yet one of them . . . am I opening an old wound? . . . one was a disapointment.
Mrs Hand (*amazed, clutching Marion's hand*) Yes!
Marion The one you loved the best.
Mrs Hand 'Tis true.
Marion (*smirking at Conroy*) And that child broke your heart.
Mrs Hand She did, she did!
Conroy (*a bellow of scorn*) Hah!
Rooney Mrs Hand, ma'am, don't mind them . . . they're trick-acting.
Mrs Hand Hold your tongue, child, this is grown-ups' talk. You have it all before ye. (*To Marion*) Talk to me, love, if you've no-one else . . . sure 'twill be a gossip.
Conroy (*to Marion*) You are an evil woman!
Mrs Hand Is that him?
Marion Sssh.

She talks to Mrs Hand as if to a confidante, but makes sure that Conroy hears

I stood by him, Mom. All through the bad times, I was by his side, his tender comrade. When the going got tough, it didn't matter . . . we were together. I was his buddy.

Conroy Oh, yuck.

Marion Those were the happy years. Then he became successful. He's famous now. At first I was so proud of him ... in his field he has treated the most eminent asses in this country.

Mrs Hand Is he a vet?

Marion Sort of. We have a nice house, we travel, we live high off the hog. I'm in the whisper-bracket. (*Whispering*) "That woman is Mrs G. P. Conroy!" So bully for me. Except that I'm not important to him any more.

Mrs Hand Ye creature.

Marion What use am I? He's made it. Who needs a rickety ladder when they're on the roof? I feel old ahead of my time.

Mrs Hand And tell, how long is it ye're married?

Marion How long? Today is our fifteenth anniversary. I'm thirty-eight.

Mrs Hand (*shocked*) Oh, my God.

Marion I know.

Mrs Hand Thirty-eight ...

Marion I look like I'm in "Lost Horizon".

Conroy (*half to himself*) I'll put a stop to this.

Olivia Dr Conroy ... no.

Conroy (*addressing himself to Mrs Hand*) Pardon me, Mrs ... uh, madam. You are the victim of a stupid hoax. This woman is——

Marion (*getting in first*) Sometimes I think he'd like to disown me.

Mrs Hand Not at all.

Conroy This woman is not my wife.

Marion (*wailing*) You see?

Mrs Hand Too true I see. (*Looking disgustedly at Conroy*) Oh, 'tis an old saying and a true one: the browner the trout the thinner the thatch.

Conroy Pardon?

Mrs Hand And let him have me sacked out of this for saying it, but he wouldn't treat the sickest of his asses the way he's treated you.

Marion No, you're wrong. George is not an evil person.

Conroy (*heavily*) Thank you.

Marion (*charmingly*) You're welcome, George. (*To Mrs Hand*) I want to be fair to my husband. I felt I owed it to him to figure out what's gone wrong with our marriage, and that's what I sat down and did. He went Park Avenue.

Conroy Where?

Marion Big-headed, darling.

Conroy Me?

Marion (*to Mrs Hand*) George and himself have always been the best of friends. But now it's got to the point where they're sleeping together.

Mrs Hand takes a look at Conroy. She says nothing, but takes rosary beads from her pinafore pocket and sits with them entwined around her fist

Conroy I think I'm beginning to cop on. It's not *my* marriage that's bothering you, it's *yours*. George ... your George, he was the one with the smell of himself.

Marion How many clubs do you belong to?
Conroy Clubs?
Marion The snooty kind . . . yacht club, golf club, tennis club, club-club. How many?
Conroy None of your business.
Marion Ten, George? A dozen?
Conroy Find out. (*Then*) Yes, I'm a member of one or two . . . what of it? I meet other professional men. We relax, we exchange views——
Marion And you drum up trade.
Conroy We do what?
Marion You advertise, baby, in neon lights.
Conroy Liar . . .
Marion I never saw the doctor who didn't. But you, George, you're the greatest. Put you in a club house, and you twinkle at every fat broad in sight. I've seen you charm them right out of their pants.

Mrs Hands eyes close. The beads and her lips begin to move

Conroy (*to Mrs Hand*) Yes? I can't hear.
Marion She's taking inventory. They can't wait for the touch of those magical hands. George, why are women so crazy about doctors? (*Playfully*) Maybe because it's the only way they can have an intimate relationship with a man without worrying why he doesn't take his socks off. (*She looks at Conroy's scowling face*) Come on, smile at me, George . . . Smile charmingly. Or do I have to get a pain in my butt first?
Conroy The kind of doctor you need will want to look higher up.
Marion (*mockingly*) At my heart? I used to keep your books; now you employ an accountant. I used to answer the door; now you have a receptionist. It's not that I mind being unused: what burns me up is feeling useless. (*To Mrs Hand*) Mom, do you know how long it's been since I was utilized for *anything*? Three months.
Mrs Hand (*blankly*) Do you tell me?
Marion I mean, since he's laid a finger on me.
Conroy (*a yelp of outrage*) Have you no shame?
Mrs Hand (*getting the message*) You're never serious?
Marion *Three months.*
Mrs Hand Sacred Heart.
Marion So how about that?
Mrs Hand Well, maybe there's some good in him after all.
Conroy (*to Marion*) Now you see here, Mrs Whatever-your-name-is . . .
Marion Conroy.
Conroy If you persist in waging some insane vendetta against me, you might at least leave this woman out of it. She's done you no harm. She's a simple, good-natured——
Mrs Hand (*suddenly*) I wasn't wanted either.
Marion Pardon me?
Mrs Hand Himself . . . he'd no time for me.

They stare at her. She continues as if in quiet contemplation

Ah, he had at first . . . love and the newness. Then it was off out with him and into a pub, or to a race meeting or a match. And if he hadn't money in his pocket, there was always a wall in the town that needed holding up. Any place but where myself was. He'd come home at night like a ticket-of-leave man back to jail . . . The ground pulling at his boots. Maybe we'd used up all the talk we'd in us, was that it? I was no more to him than a picture of someone dead . . . up on the wall that he never looked at. I stayed with him. I waited till the children were off and fending for themselves. Then I went.

Marion You left him?

Mrs Hand (*again*) I went. If I wouldn't throw out an old dress for a skirt that could be made over, why would I throw away a life? And I always did a day's work, only now I'm paid for it.

Marion (*admiringly*) Mom, you're my kind of lady. Shake.

She extends her hand. Mrs Hand rises and moves away

Mrs Hand Shake hands, how are you!

Marion Why not?

Mrs Hand I have the leavings of my life all to myself now. A slave to no man and a fool to all of them.

Marion A fool? Are you kidding?

Mrs Hand A hard road is bad. No road is nothing.

Marion You had the guts to walk out . . .

Mrs Hand And I rue the day. Ah, the man was hopeless . . . fierce. But whatever the heartache, by yourself is the worst of all. I thrun away the one poor thing I had left. 'Tis gone, and now I have no-one to turn his back on me. (*To Marion, with burning urgency*) That's why you won't leave him. You mustn't. Now say you won't.

Marion (*embarrassed, contrite*) Look, Mom . . . No, not Mom any more, I don't mean that . . .

Mrs Hand You'll give him a second chance . . . yes, you will.

Marion Please . . .

Mrs Hand He'll make it up to you. Isn't he the best in the world?

Marion Please listen to me. We owe you . . . no, goddammit, *I* owe you an apology.

Mrs Hand (*not heeding*) On my knees I beg you. You'll destroy yourself and for nothing. Stay with him.

Marion I'm sorry, dear, I really honest-to-God am, but what this gentleman says is true. It's all been a stupid game that went wrong, and it's my fault.

Mrs Hand A game?

Marion He and I . . . I don't know how to explain this, but we——

Conroy is at her side. He puts his arm around her shoulder

Conroy What my wife is trying to say—and very badly—is that we're staying together.

Marion glances at him, stunned. He is a new Conroy, solicitous, kindly

And thank you, you've been very kind. If ... uh, if Marion will overlook my behaviour and give me another chance, I'll do my best to make it up to her. I haven't been a considerate husband, but from now on I'll try.

Mrs Hand (*hardly believing*) You're saying it to please me.

Conroy I mean it.

Mrs Hand (*to Marion*) And yourself? Ye'll not leave him?

Marion (*nervously*) Leave George? That'll be the day.

Mrs Hand Thanks be to God. Oh, 'tis what I always say and 'tis true: the longer the fast, the sweeter the thrush.

Marion You said a——Could you repeat that?

Mrs Hand is suddenly overcome by tears of sheer happiness

Mrs Hand Will you look at me ... making a show of myself. I need a breath of fresh air ... I'll go back and sit in the hot press. (*As tears well up again*) God bless and keep the pair of ye. (*She takes a final look at Marion*) And may the saints pity her ... only thirty-eight.

She goes out

Marion (*to Conroy*) You are a nice man.

Conroy (*not severely*) And you are an American idiot.

Marion I'll drink to that. I am also a louse, a skunk and a rat fink. (*Extending her hand*) Now that we've cleared that up, I'm going to get my hand shook today if it kills me.

Conroy (*hesitating*) No more tricks?

Marion Scout's honour.

Conroy And no more games?

Marion You got it.

As he makes to take her hand

Except ...

Conroy (*leaping back as if stung*) No! Except nothing. You keep away from me.

Marion All I was going to——

Conroy Get back!

The telephone on the desk rings. They all stare at it, including Rooney

Rooney (*picking up the receiver*) Thanks be to Jasus. (*Into the phone*) Who's that? ... Yes, yes, 'tis me. What ... ?

Marion (*to Conroy*) Keep your hair on. Now that we're friends, I was only going to ask your advice. About Eleanor.

Conroy About ... ?

Olivia rises and smiles at Conroy

Rooney (*into the phone*) The corner of Kildare Street. ... I have ye. (*He looks at his watch*) Three minutes, so. ... Oh, I will, on the dot.

As he drops his voice to a whisper, Conroy, bristling with impatience, comes and stands over him

Listen, you won't credit it. I have a pair here forenenst me astray in the head. Loonies. I think they got over the shaggin' wall of some——(*He sees Conroy. Aloud*) I'll do that for ye, so. Sound man. God bless.
Conroy (*glaring*) Well?
Rooney Grand.
Conroy Did that call have to do with us?
Rooney (*flustered*) The ... the marchers are on time to the tick and they'll be handing in the petition at Leinster House at half-past three.
Conroy It's nearly that now. Then what?
Rooney Nothing ... the pubs'll be open. You'll want to fill in the form and pay your deposit. Wait, now.

He finds a rental form and gives it to Conroy, who takes it to a table and sets about filling it in. Rooney waves a second form at Marion

Missis ...
Marion (*looking at Conroy*) We already filled ours in, didn't we, Olly?
Olivia (*to Rooney, but looking at Conroy*) It's on your desk.

Rooney finds the completed form and stamps it, then again looks at his watch as if under starter's orders

Marion (*to Conroy*) You're as sharp as a tack, you know that? You were right about George ... *my* George. You were on the ball, because yes, he did have a lady fair.
Conroy (*mumbling*) "Previous experience ..." None.
Marion For all I know he may have played the field. But this was big league stuff ... World Series. Name of Eleanor.
Conroy "Probable destination ..." Nowhere.
Marion She scared me. Eleanor had the one quality that every married woman fears. She was single.

As Conroy pays her no attention

Hey, Doc ... you with me?
Conroy Sorry, but as soon as I get this filled in I have to rescue my wife from that dosshouse that calls itself an hotel. So if you don't mind ...

Marion goes to the relief map

Marion Where were George and I then on life's river? Twenty years along it. (*Peering*) About here ... Banagher. Say, Olly, doesn't that come into one of those cute Irish sayings of yours?
Olivia Does it? Oh, yes ... "That bangs Banagher."
Marion That's the one. And George was banging Eleanor. Well, I knew there had to be another woman because he was putting on weight.
Conroy "Four-berth or six-berth ..." (*Then*) Putting on weight?
Marion Sure. That's one of the drawbacks of adultery. It comes from eating two dinners. Well, it didn't take me long to find out who she was. Telephone calls ... letters.
Conroy Oh?
Marion There weren't any.

Conroy (*at sea*) Ah.
Marion Want to know what I did?

Conroy gives a quick empty smile and goes back to his form

I thought about no telephone calls and no letters and what that meant, and one day I went downstairs, which was reserved for George's professional work, and I said: "I am Hercule Poirot, and someone in this house is a——
Conroy (*reading*) "Single screw . . ."
Marion Right! Tell you the truth, that wasn't exactly what I said. What I did say was . . . (*sweetly*) "Eleanor, honey . . ."

Olivia comes forward as Eleanor

Olivia Yes, Marion?
Marion Take a seat, dear. I thought we might have a chat.
Olivia If you like.
Marion Oh, I like. My, you're a pretty girl.
Olivia Thank you.
Marion And smart. And so trim and self-possessed . . . and single. Have you ever thought of marriage, Eleanor?
Olivia Marriage?
Marion You know . . . that thing where if you can hold on to your husband for twenty years, you get to keep him. Ever thought about it?
Olivia Once or twice. But there's still plenty of time, and besides there's no-one who's——
Marion Single?
Olivia Special, I was going to say.
Marion (*lazily*) Say it then, what the hell. What's important is, you're having a ball. You . . . uh, enjoy working under George? (*She stresses the "under" hardly noticeably*)
Olivia Oh, I do. (*Gushing*) He's so . . . I suppose the word is "brilliant".
Marion That's one of the words.
Olivia To be part of his work, even the smallest, most unimportant part, makes me feel somehow . . .
Marion Fulfilled?
Olivia Yes!
Marion Mm. Remind me . . . how long is it you've been with him?
Olivia Four years.
Marion No, I don't mean that. I don't mean as his secretary . . . I mean, how long have you been screwing him?

This has the effect of causing Conroy and Rooney to look up sharply

Or maybe it's *been* four years . . . what do I know? Maybe on that very first day he said: "Come in, Miss McNulty, and bring your notebook and a condom."
Olivia (*shocked*) Marion!
Marion No, my guess is it began a year ago, around the time he stopped calling you "dear" and "darling" in front of me.

Rooney picks up the telephone and starts dialling surreptitiously

When people who like each other a lot start getting formal, I start wondering what else they're getting. Want to hear something else? George became a smiler. We'd be going to bed, and he'd stand there with one leg out of his shorts, and there was this . . . smile on his face. He's married and he's smiling. *Why?*

Olivia Marion, this is ridiculous.

Marion Is it?

Olivia I don't want to be rude——

Marion (*hard*) Then don't be. Don't get up on that high horse with me, kiddo . . . it's a long way down. I'm telling you that I know about you and George. Now are you going to deny it or do I give you proof? Real proof.

Olivia is silent. Rooney gets his telephone connection

Rooney (*into the phone, his voice low*) That you, Mossy? . . . Mossy, it's me . . . Fergal. What's a comdom? (*sic*)

Olivia No, it's true. I don't want real proof.

Marion That's good, because there isn't any. I wasn't sure.

Olivia Oh.

Rooney (*into the phone*) Well, Jasus, find out. (*Hanging up*) Ignorance, ignorance.

Marion (*wryly, sing-song*) I fooled you!

Olivia Yes, you did. Well, now that it's out in the open, I want to be honest.

Marion You're a sweetheart.

Olivia Neither of us ever intended it to happen. George and I——

Marion I don't care. I don't care what George feels about you or what you feel about him. I don't care if you played the death scene from *Camille* in broad daylight and sold tickets. All I want is your can out of here.

Olivia Well, if you're going to be vulgar——

Marion You bet your sweet ass I'm going to be vulgar. Because if you are not out of here in twenty-four hours flat, you know what I'm going to do? I'm going to walk into George's waiting room with all those people sitting around, and I'm going to say: "Good-morning, Eleanor baby, did you screw my husband again last night? How was it? Was it good for you? Did the earth move? Did you come?" I'm going to do that, and I'm going to keep on doing it.

Olivia You wouldn't dare.

Marion Me? Don't you know who I am? I am a vulgar, brash, loud American . . . a Catholic redneck from Detroit, Michigan. We don't have manners or refinement, we don't know from nothing. You think I'm going to fight you for my husband? By your rules . . . teacups at dawn? Crap, kiddo. I'm going to kick your tight little keester right out of here, starting now. So how do you like them apples?

Olivia If I go, George will——

Marion Stay right where he is and take it out on me. I'm not even going to tell him we had this conversation. You tell him.

Olivia I will.

Marion You do that.
Olivia I mean it.
Marion Fine! (*She steps out of the playlet and into the present*) Fine. That was just fine, Olly dear. Thank you. (*To Conroy*) Maybe she did tell him ... I don't know. Eleanor went, and George and I never discussed it. Oh, I meant we should kick it around one day when we were old and folksy and too comfortable to care. Funny thing ... that day never comes. Then George bought the farm.
Conroy The farm?
Marion (*jabbing a thumb upwards*) Heavenly Acres. So I never did get to find out.

Conroy looks at her quizzically

What it was that made Eleanor so all-fired special. Why he went to her for the answers I thought I'd given him. I'd be obligated for your opinion.
Conroy (*again a quick, blank smile*) Don't have one. (*He signs his name with a flourish and rises from the table*)
Marion (*quietly*) Come on Doc, you're holding out.
Conroy I never knew your late husband. I don't even know the sort of man he was.
Marion You knew him.
Conroy When?
Marion You knew him like I know your wife ... that little lady who's sitting on the edge of the bed right now waiting for you to come get her. I look inside of me and I find her. Part of her.
Conroy I don't think George and I have that much in common.
Marion Not even Eleanor?
Conroy (*a moment's pause*) Never heard of her.
Marion Don't get mad. I wasn't insinuating ... school's out now. What I'm trying to say is, if there *was* an Eleanor in your life ... *why*? Maybe because she's young and your wife isn't?
Conroy (*firmly*) No.
Marion Why, then? Because she's pretty and smart and new, and her body is good?
Conroy (*stronger*) No.
Marion What else is there? Maybe she's fantastic in the sack, is that it?
Conroy Maybe George got tired.
Marion Do you mean of me? (*Shrugging*) Sure. I'll buy that.
Conroy No, not of you ... of something that's so natural to you, to every damn one of you, that you don't even notice it. Of *scoring points*. You ... you like to play games, right? Well, this knocks your kind of game into a cocked hat ... only there isn't any winner, because it never stops.
Marion Scoring ... points?
Conroy And we have to play it. George and I have to play it, because if we don't play, we go under. But we get tired: you have more stamina than we do. So maybe that's the reason for Eleanor. George just needed a rest.
Marion Him? He never played a game in his life.
Conroy No?

Marion Who ... George?
Conroy (*suddenly*) There's no salt on the table.
Marion What?
Conroy I said, Marion, you forgot the salt.
Marion Did I? (*Then*) Wait a minute ... sure. George says I forgot the salt, and I say ... "Go get it yourself."
Conroy No. You fetch the salt.
Marion (*his pupil*) I fetch the salt.
Conroy (*prompting*) And later on ...?
Marion Later on I——(*She sees the pattern*) There's egg on your lip.
Conroy (*wiping it off*) Is there?
Marion Yecch.
Conroy All gone?
Marion And you left the kitchen window open last night.

This last game begins casually, then escalates in speed and intensity to rage and mutual loathing. From his desk, Rooney looks on with mounting alarm

Conroy Did I?
Marion We could have been murdered in our sleep.
Conroy Sorry.
Marion Don't be. I forgot the salt and you forgot the kitchen window. Now we're quits.
Conroy Even Steven.
Marion Only we could have had our throats cut.
Conroy I did apologize. I should have closed the window and I forgot. (*Fatally*) I was tired.
Marion I get tired, too.
Conroy I know.
Marion I don't think you do know. Maybe in your book, in that encyclopaedia of yours, this house runs itself.
Conroy You work hard, I agree.
Marion That's damn white of you, George.
Conroy And I do, too.
Marion Sure you do ... it accounts for your dishpan hands. Only I can't afford to take afternoons off.
Conroy When do I ever take——
Marion A week last Tuesday!
Conroy Did I?
Marion Three hours and ... (*being noble*) I'm not the sort of woman who counts minutes.
Conroy Count them, count them. I had no appointments, so I went to play a few sets at Fitzwilliam.
Marion If that's where you say you went.
Conroy I'm telling you that's where I went.
Marion Then I believe you.
Conroy I was in——
Marion Who cares!
Conroy Fitzbloodywilliam!

She shrugs, a woman wronged

Come to that, you go out, too. You have your coffee mornings, you meet your friends . . .
Marion Why shouldn't I go out? You want me to stay indoors?
Conroy No, all I'm——
Marion Cooped up in this Alcatraz?
Conroy It happens to be our home.
Marion It happens to be my prison. Christ, now he begrudges me one cup of stinking coffee.
Conroy Since when?
Marion One lousy cup.
Conroy You can drink coffee until it——
Marion And a Danish pastry. As for my seeing the very few friends that thanks to you I have left . . . well, that of course is what you cannot stand.
Conroy Is that a fact?
Marion That is a fact. You don't want me to have a life of my own. It burns you up. If you had any guts, it would stick in them. Well, I have news for you. From here on in, I go where I like.
Conroy Go, then . . . go.
Marion I see . . . now you want to be rid of me. Well, the Woman in the Iron Mask is free at last, you know that? Damn you, George, I've been the doormat in this house all my life. I waited on you, slaved for you, and I reared your children. You didn't rear 'em . . . I did.

She goes to where Rooney is sitting and drags him upright from his chair by the collar

(*Shaking Rooney at George*) George, take a look at your son.
Rooney Easy . . . easy . . .
Marion He's everything a father could dream of . . . upright, honest, cultivated.
Rooney Jasus, let go.
Marion A young Adonis. Six foot two . . . an athlete, he can have any girl he likes. They grovel at his feet. As for brains, he is brilliant . . . and it's thanks to me, because you never cared about him, you were never here.
Conroy That's a lie.
Marion (*to Rooney*) Are you listening, darling? Your father never even liked you.
Conroy You evil old bag.
Marion He hated you.
Rooney Gerroff.
Marion (*to Conroy*) Monster.
Conroy Superbitch.
Marion Psychopath.
Conroy Cow.
Marion Pig.
Conroy American.
Marion Ohhh!

*In her revulsion, she lets go of Rooney, who goes fleeing from reception, pulling
a whistle from his pocket. He reaches the jetty and blows three piercing blasts*

Rooney Come on ... for Chrissakes will ye come in!

*Meanwhile, Conroy and Marion stand as if frozen, glaring with intense
loathing at each other. Then their features slowly relax and soften until they
are smiling. Rooney returns, panting*

They're on the way. (*To Conroy*) Excuse me ... I say they're coming.
Have you it filled in? I say, have you your form?

Conroy (*to Marion*) Did you fill in a form?

Marion Yes, we filled in a form.

Conroy Do I need to fill in a form?

Marion No, you don't need to fill in a form.

Conroy crushes his form into a ball and throws it away

Rooney Ye can't do that. If ye want to hire a boat——

Conroy |
Marion | (*together; without looking at him*) Cruiser.

Rooney —ye have to fill a form in.

Conroy Why don't we go out and see our ship come in?

Marion Why don't we?

They go out on the jetty

Rooney (*feebly*) 'Tis against the rules. (*To Olivia*) Where are they going?
What are they at?

Olivia I love them. Aren't they incredible? They do this every anniversary.

*Marion and Conroy, his arm around her shoulder, stand looking off at the
lake. The sound of a diesel engine is heard. A ship's hooter blows*

CURTAIN

A VIEW FROM THE OBELISK

FURNITURE AND PROPERTY LIST

On stage: Bench set in alcove at base of obelisk
Grass
Outcrops of stone

Off stage: Drawing pad, pencil **(Eoghain)**

LIGHTING PLOT

Property fittings required: *nil*

Exterior. A hilltop

To open: General exterior lighting—afternoon

No cues

FURNITURE AND PROPERTY LIST

On stage: 2 basket-chairs
Small table. *On it:* table lamp

Personal: **Mrs Slade:** handbag with money, gloves
Mrs Ansley: bag with knitting, gloves

LIGHTING PLOT

Practical fitting required: table lamp

Exterior. A terrace

To open: General exterior lighting—mid-afternoon

Cue 1   **Mrs Slade:** "... and here we sit and——"   (Page 28)
Begin slow fade as sun sets

Cue 2   **Head Waiter** switches on table lamp   (Page 30)
Snap on table lamp and covering spot

EFFECTS PLOT

Cue 1   **Mrs Slade:** "... and here we sit and——"   (Page 28)
Bell chimes 4 o'clock, with other bells joining in

PIZZAZZ

FURNITURE AND PROPERTY LIST

On stage: Desk. *On it:* forms, stamp and ink-pad, telephone, flower-vase, newspaper
Sofa
Chairs
Small tables. *On them:* brochures, boating magazines
On walls: plans and drawings of cruisers, large relief map of the River
Shannon
Holiday baggage, including a hamper containing a paper plate, serviette,
cellophane-wrapped sandwiches, flask of coffee

Off stage: Pile of bed-linen, towels **(Mrs Hand)**

Personal: **Marion:** bag containing pack of cards, £1 in pocket
Rooney: wrist-watch, whistle in pocket
Conroy: wrist-watch, pen
Mrs Hand: wedding ring, rosary beads in pocket

LIGHTING PLOT

Interior and exterior. A reception area and a jetty

Property fittings required: *nil*

To open: General interior lighting on reception area, general exterior
lighting on jetty—afternoon

No cues

EFFECTS PLOT

Cue 1	As CURTAIN rises *Cruiser's diesel engine, off*	(Page 41)
Cue 2	**Marion:** "... your ti-em is up!" *Engine fades as cruiser moves out*	(Page 41)
Cue 3	**Conroy:** "Get back!" *Telephone rings*	(Page 67)
Cue 4	**Marion** and **Conroy** stand looking off at the lake *Cruiser's diesel engine, off; ship's hooter blows*	(Page 74)

www.ingramcontent.com/pod-product-compliance
Lightning Source LLC
LaVergne TN
LVHW051757080426
835511LV00018B/3344